Physical Fitness Standards to Support Readiness and Deployability

An Examination of Department of the Air Force Policies and Culture

MIRIAM MATTHEWS, CARRA S. SIMS, SEAN ROBSON, MATTHEW WALSH, STEPHANIE RENNANE, JOSHUA SNOKE

Prepared for the Department of the Air Force
Approved for public release; distribution unlimited

PROJECT AIR FORCE

For more information on this publication, visit **www.rand.org/t/RRA552-2**.

About RAND

The RAND Corporation is a research organization that develops solutions to public policy challenges to help make communities throughout the world safer and more secure, healthier and more prosperous. RAND is nonprofit, nonpartisan, and committed to the public interest. To learn more about RAND, visit www.rand.org.

Research Integrity

Our mission to help improve policy and decisionmaking through research and analysis is enabled through our core values of quality and objectivity and our unwavering commitment to the highest level of integrity and ethical behavior. To help ensure our research and analysis are rigorous, objective, and nonpartisan, we subject our research publications to a robust and exacting quality-assurance process; avoid both the appearance and reality of financial and other conflicts of interest through staff training, project screening, and a policy of mandatory disclosure; and pursue transparency in our research engagements through our commitment to the open publication of our research findings and recommendations, disclosure of the source of funding of published research, and policies to ensure intellectual independence. For more information, visit www.rand.org/about/principles.

RAND's publications do not necessarily reflect the opinions of its research clients and sponsors.

Published by the RAND Corporation, Santa Monica, Calif.
© 2022 RAND Corporation
RAND® is a registered trademark.

Library of Congress Cataloging-in-Publication Data is available for this publication.
ISBN: 978-1-9774-0904-1

Cover: U.S. Air Force photo by Airman 1st Class Isaac O. Guest IV.

Limited Print and Electronic Distribution Rights

About This Report

Building a more comprehensive understanding of how different factors influence exercise habits, test preparation, and the perceived importance of fitness is critical to promoting a ready and deployable force. Therefore, the Department of the Air Force (DAF) engaged the RAND Corporation to evaluate the validity and perceived relevance of the U.S. Air Force's (AF's) fitness assessment (FA) to support the readiness and deployability of airmen and guardians by examining the possible impact of the AF-FA on military career and future military health experience.

To address this objective, we examined the empirical associations between AF-FA scores and various health-related and professional outcomes. We also conducted interviews with DAF commanders and military personnel to identify perceptions of current policies, objectives, communication, and leadership support for fitness and exercise. During the production of this report, the DAF made changes to the AF-FA, which are not reflected in our data analysis or interviews with subject-matter experts.

The research reported here was commissioned by the AF's Force Management Policy Directorate (AF/A1P) and conducted within the Workforce, Development, and Health Program of RAND Project AIR FORCE as part of a fiscal year 2020 project, "Fitness Standards to Support Readiness and Deployability."

The RAND Corporation is committed to the ethical and respectful treatment of RAND research participants and complies with all applicable laws and regulations, including the Federal Policy for the Protection of Human Subjects, also known as the "Common Rule." The research described in this report was screened and, if necessary, reviewed by RAND's Human Subjects Protection Committee, which serves as RAND's institutional review board (IRB) charged with ensuring the ethical treatment of individuals who are participants in RAND projects through observation, intervention, interaction, or use of data about them. RAND's Federalwide Assurance (FWA) for the Protection of Human Subjects (FWA00003425, effective until June 22, 2023) serves as our assurance of compliance with federal regulations.

The views of any unnamed sources are solely their own and do not represent the official policy or position of any department or agency of the U.S. government.

RAND Project AIR FORCE

RAND Project AIR FORCE (PAF), a division of the RAND Corporation, is the Department of the Air Force's (DAF's) federally funded research and development center for studies and analyses, supporting both the United States Air Force and the United States Space Force. PAF provides the DAF with independent analyses of policy alternatives affecting the development, employment, combat readiness, and support of current and future air, space, and cyber forces. Research is conducted in four programs: Strategy and Doctrine; Force Modernization and Employment; Resource Management; and Workforce, Development, and Health. The research reported here was prepared under contract FA7014-16-D-1000.

Additional information about PAF is available on our website:
www.rand.org/paf/

This report documents work originally shared with the DAF on March 22, 2021. The draft report, issued on June 4, 2021, was reviewed by formal peer reviewers and DAF subject-matter experts.

Acknowledgments

We are grateful for the support of Brig Gen Troy E. Dunn, Director, Military Force Management Policy, Deputy Chief of Staff for Manpower, Personnel and Services, Headquarters U.S. Air Force (AF/A1P). Our primary contacts in AF/A1P were Col Jennifer Allee, Lt Col Matthew Huibregtse, and Emi Izawa. We very much appreciate their willingness to provide policy background and contact information that was important for the data-gathering effort related to this research.

Personnel data related to career outcomes were very important for our analysis, and we are grateful to David Schulker, Mike Schiefer, Perry Firoz, and Anthony Lawrence for their help with relevant variables and data. We are grateful for the assistance of Teague Ruder and Linda Cottrell with health outcomes and data preparation. We also thank those who assisted with qualitative data collection and cleaning, namely Sarah Weilant, Yuliya Shokh, and Rick Garvey.

This study would not have been possible without the willing participation of officers and enlisted personnel in our hour-long interview about fitness standards. Their candid observations and important considerations related to the current and future implementation of the FA will help the AF determine how best to use fitness standards. Because we promised interviews their anonymity, we can only thank them collectively, but we hope that we have represented their individual views adequately in this report.

Finally, we thank Nelson Lim, director of RAND Project AIR FORCE's Workforce, Development, and Health Program, for his support throughout this project. We also thank Maria Lytell, Charles Engel, and Tracy Kreuger for their helpful comments, which improved the report's presentation.

Contents

Figures

Tables

Summary

Issue

To ensure military personnel have the requisite physical fitness to serve, the Department of the Air Force (DAF) has established a variety of medical and physical standards. For example, the Tier 1 fitness assessment (FA) is intended to minimize health risks among airmen and support an "active lifestyle." It includes four component fitness scores: a 1.5-mile run or 2.0-kilometer walk, designed to measure cardiorespiratory fitness; an abdominal circumference (AC) measurement for body composition; and push-ups and sit-ups, which assess muscular fitness. This study focused on evaluating data relevant to the Tier 1 FA to determine whether FA components meet their intended purpose to minimize health risks and maximize readiness of airmen.

Approach

To examine fitness, we analyzed extracts from the Air Force Fitness Management System that contained complete data from all U.S. Air Force (AF) FAs completed by active duty officers and enlisted personnel from fiscal year (FY) 2005 to FY 2018. To explore the relationship between component fitness scores and career outcomes, we derived variables from the Military Personnel Data System and other Air Force Personnel Center data sources (i.e., administrative data sources routinely collected and used for unit and service member accountability and promotion management). To explore the relationship between component fitness scores and health outcomes, we integrated Defense Health Agency databases from the Military Health System Data Repository to create an analytic file of health outcomes that provides a picture of all health care received in inpatient and outpatient settings at both military treatment facilities (MTFs) and outside of MTFs (derived from TRICARE claims data). We also examined perceptions of the DAF's culture of fitness by conducting 35 semi-structured telephone interviews with DAF active duty officers and enlisted personnel in squadron types of interest to the sponsor.

Key Findings About the Air Force Tier 1 Fitness Assessment

AF-FA Components Are Associated with Positive Effects for Career and Health

Looking at the relationship between AF-FA components and career outcomes, we found the following:

- Although the average body mass index (BMI) of airmen has increased from FY 2005 to FY 2018, waist-to-height ratio, a different measure of body composition that may be more suitable for fit populations, has decreased. Additionally, the average aerobic and muscular fitness of airmen have increased. These results suggest that airmen fitness has improved over time.
- Multiple fitness components are positively associated with annual retention and physical eligibility for deployment, and the strength of association is greatest for aerobic fitness, as assessed by the 1.5-mile run.
- Likewise, multiple fitness components are positively associated with early- and mid-career outcomes, and the strength of association is again greatest for aerobic fitness.
- These associations span multiple years: Fitness in the very first year of service (YOS) predicted annual and career outcomes over the first ten YOS.

Next, in terms of the relationship between AF-FA components and health outcomes, our results showed that

- AC and the 1.5-mile run are important components for reducing the risk of different health diagnoses.
- Sit-ups and push-ups were also associated with health outcomes, but they were not as strong or consistent as that of the 1.5-mile run.
- The relationship between fitness and injury diagnoses was inconsistent.

Perceptions of the Fitness Assessment and the Broader Culture of Fitness Are Mixed

We also sought to examine airmen's perceptions of current fitness policies and the culture of fitness across the DAF. Overall, our interview results suggest that

- Interviewees do not understand why they must complete the AF-FA or why any of the AF-FA components have been included in the assessment.
- There is a great deal of variability in perceptions of the AF-FA and its components, with some perceiving the standards as too strict and others perceiving them as too lenient.
- Interviewees indicated that finding time to exercise is a barrier to fitness, and they proposed that providing time during the duty day to work out and regular unit physical training could assist with addressing this barrier.

Recommendations

Drawing from our results, we provide several recommendations to improve the rationale for and the validity and acceptance of the AF-FA:

- Ensure airmen understand why they are required to complete the AF-FA and the purpose of each of its components.
  - Consider whether and how to provide information to airmen and guardians about their predicted health-related risks based on their AF-FA scores.
- Continue measuring, recording, and reporting AC data.

Abbreviations

AC	abdominal circumference
AF	U.S. Air Force
AFFMS	Air Force Fitness Management System
AFI	Air Force Instruction
AFPC	Air Force Personnel Center
AFSC	Air Force specialty code
BMI	body mass index
CCS	clinical classifications software
CDC	Centers for Disease Control and Prevention
DAF	Department of the Air Force
DHA	Defense Health Agency
FA	fitness assessment
FY	fiscal year
ICD	International Classification of Diseases
MilPDS	Military Personnel Data System
MTF	military treatment facility
PT	physical training
SOS	squadron officer school
WHtR	waist-to-height ratio
YOS	year(s) of service

1. Introduction

Military readiness requires service members to be mentally and physically fit in order to perform mission- and job-related duties in a wide range of environments. To ensure military personnel have the requisite physical fitness to serve, fitness standards can be designed to promote general health and well-being and ensure that service members can meet situation-specific physical demands. These various objectives are defined by different tiers of fitness (see Figure 1.1).

Figure 1.1. General Conceptualization of Fitness Tiers

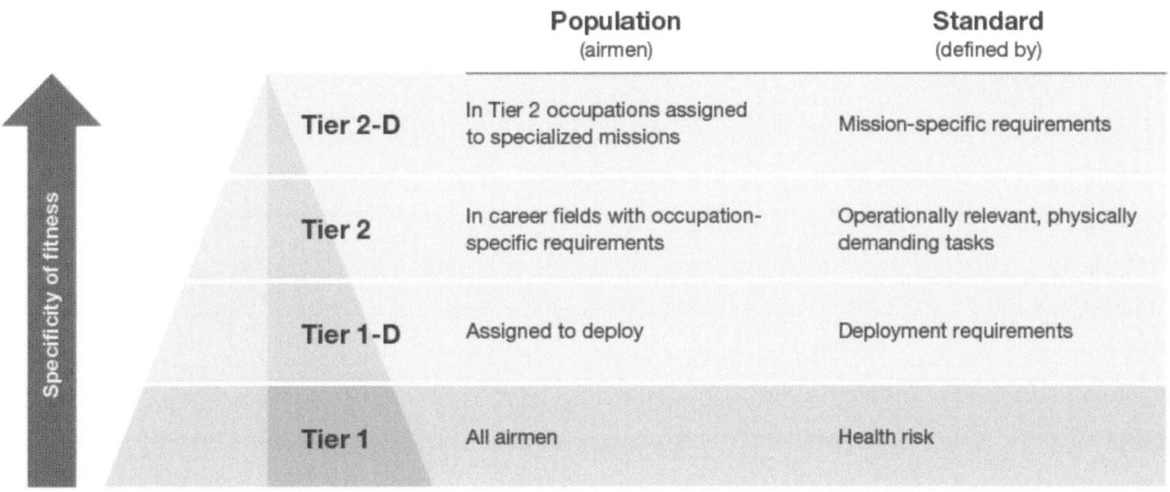

	Population (airmen)	Standard (defined by)
Tier 2-D	In Tier 2 occupations assigned to specialized missions	Mission-specific requirements
Tier 2	In career fields with occupation-specific requirements	Operationally relevant, physically demanding tasks
Tier 1-D	Assigned to deploy	Deployment requirements
Tier 1	All airmen	Health risk

Specificity of fitness (increasing, shown by upward arrow)

SOURCE: Robson et al., 2017; Palmer et al., 2000.

The Department of the Air Force (DAF) has established physical fitness standards to address Tiers 1 and 2, but it does not currently have predeployment standards (Tier 1-D) or mission-specific fitness requirements (Tier 2-D). The DAF's occupationally specific and relevant Tier 2 fitness tests and standards affect fewer than 25 percent of Air Force specialties codes (AFSCs).[1] However, the DAF implements Tier 1 fitness tests and standards for the entire DAF, across all AFSCs (Air Force Manual [AFMAN] 36-2905, 2020). The intent of Tier 1 fitness tests and standards is to minimize health risks among airmen and guardians. Indeed, AFMAN 36-2905 notes that the intent of the fitness program is to support an active lifestyle, which "increases productivity, optimizes health, and decreases absenteeism while maintaining a higher level of readiness" (p. 6). Thus, in this report, we focus on exploring the relationships between the AF-

---

[1] For an example, see Air Force Guidance Memorandum 2018-36-02, 2018.

1

FA components to career and health outcomes and examining airmen's perceptions of the Tier 1 AF-FA and the broader culture of fitness across the DAF.

Background and Motivation

The Air Force Fitness Assessment

The AF-FA is governed by Air Force Instruction (AFI) 36-2905, *Air Force Physical Fitness Program*. The FA consists of four fitness components:

- Aerobic fitness assessment. Airmen perform a 1.5-mile run. Those medically exempted from the run may be cleared for an alternate aerobic assessment (e.g., a 2.0-kilometer walk).
- Body stature and mass. Height and weight measures are obtained, and the airmen's AC has traditionally been measured and incorporated as part of the AF-FA.
- Muscular fitness assessment. Airmen perform a 1-minute timed push-up test and a 1-minute timed sit-up test.

Age- and gender-based standards are set for the 1.5-mile run, AC, sit-ups, and push-ups. Performance on these four components are combined into a composite score. Airmen who receive an excellent composite score are required to test again in one year, airmen who receive a satisfactory score must test a minimum of twice per year, and airmen who receive an unsatisfactory score must test again within 90 calendar days.[2] The stated intent of these AF-FA components is to increase readiness and physical health of the force. In support of that intent, the AF has expressed a desire to establish evidence to support the validity of the standards used for each AF-FA component. The level of evidence supporting these standards currently varies. For example, scores for push-ups and sit-ups are norm-referenced and not grounded in any established relationships to career or health outcomes. Although a prior RAND study qualitatively reviewed evidence related to the overall FA (Robson et al., 2021), this study set out to evaluate the quantitative evidence for each AF-FA component.

Previous Research

General Research on Fitness and Career and Health

The links between physical fitness, exercise, and health have been well documented (Reiner et al., 2013). Indeed, the Centers for Disease Control and Prevention (CDC) has documented a wide variety of benefits from regular physical activity, including a reduction in risk for the following (U.S. Department of Health and Human Services, 2018):

---

[2] Airmen receive a composite score on a 100-point scale based on the following maximum component scores: 60 points for aerobic, 20 points for body composition, 10 points for push-ups, and 10 points for sit-ups. The composite FA scores are categorized as excellent (≥ 90 points), satisfactory (75–89.9 points), unsatisfactory (≤ 74.9 points or one or more component minimums have not been met), and exempt.

- all-cause mortality
- cardiovascular disease mortality
- cardiovascular disease (including heart disease and stroke)
- hypertension
- type 2 diabetes
- certain cancers
- depression
- anxiety.

Research has also demonstrated the positive effects of physical fitness and activity on work performance and productivity (Pronk et al., 2004), although more research is needed. More recent research has also shown that exercise and fitness can positively impact cognitive performance and may help to protect against stress (Chang et al., 2012; Forcier et al., 2006). Together, these findings suggest a strong rationale for a general health approach, as described by Tier 1 standards.

Research on the AF-FA

A 2021 evaluation of the AF-FA concluded that "the current AF-FA is a practical assessment that measures critical components of health-related fitness using well-supported assessments" (Robson et al., 2021, p. vii). However, the report's findings suggested that the DAF could take several steps to strengthen the AF-FA. For example, subject-matter experts raised concerns that push-ups and sit-ups are scored more subjectively than the other AF-FA components are, which could affect the accuracy and reliability of those component scores. Indeed, other research that reviews the test-retest reliability of muscular endurance tests indicate that they have somewhat lower and more-variable reliabilities compared with timed or distance run tests (Hauschild et al., 2014). The DAF could also strengthen the AF-FA by using its own data to establish health and readiness risk-based standards for all fitness components. Currently, the DAF uses criterion-referenced standards for the 1.5-mile run and AC based on criteria and research evidence provided by the Cooper Center Longitudinal Study, which followed 116,000 U.S. residents over time (Blair et al., 1989). Although these criteria, implemented in 2010, reflect a commitment to science-based standards, the standards for push-ups and sit-ups relied on normative data and, hence, only provide insight into airmen's relative fitness.[3] However, such standards cannot help gauge airmen's health risks or airmen's readiness for deployment or an AF career.

The AF has conducted some research studies for specific purposes or for certain populations within the DAF, but it has yet to conduct a full evaluation across the entire force. AF research to date includes studies that have focused on the relationship between fitness and basic military training injuries. In a study of over 60,000 trainees, Nye et al., 2016, found that musculoskeletal injuries incurred during training were more common among trainees who were less fit at the time

---

[3] Normative data summarize what is usual in a defined population at a specific time point.

that they entered basic military training. Male and female trainees who incurred injuries later in basic military training had performed fewer sit-ups and push-ups and took longer to complete the 1.5-mile run at the beginning of their training compared with trainees who remained uninjured throughout training. There were no differences in body composition (measured by body mass index [BMI] and AC) between injured and uninjured trainees.

Other studies suggest that FAs may play an important role in preventing metabolic syndrome—a condition linked to the subsequent development of type 2 diabetes and cardiovascular disease.[4] Active duty personnel have lower rates of metabolic syndrome compared with the general population (Ervin, 2009) and with DAF retirees in the same age range (Cranston et al., 2017). Even though the AF is comparatively more fit than the general population, excess weight contributes to increased total health care expenditures and results in lost productivity (Robbins et al., 2002).

Several questions remain, which we aim to address in this report:

- How relevant are civilian fitness results to the DAF, which has a relatively young population?
- What are the relationships between AF-FA components and health outcomes?
- Is there a link between fitness and an airman's career outcomes?
- Does the AF-FA scoring system differentiate between levels of health risk?

We evaluated over 1.5 million personnel records of active duty officers and enlisted personnel to begin to address these questions. Moreover, we consider the validity of the AF-FA and its standards as an indicator of airmen's health risks and AF career readiness.

Overview of Analytic Approach and Data Sources

To examine fitness, we analyzed extracts from various AF data systems (i.e., administrative data sources routinely collected and used by the DAF for unit and service member accountability and promotion management purposes). Specifically, we used data from the Air Force Fitness Management System (AFFMS),[5] which contained complete AF-FA data of active duty officers and enlisted personnel received from fiscal year (FY) 2005 to FY 2018.[6] The data consist of biomorphic variables (height and weight), exemptions, and raw and derived scores from the four fitness components. Because derived scores for the AF-FA components and the composite score

---

[4] Metabolic syndrome was originally a term designed to look at a preobesity condition that could serve as a clinically modifiable risk factor for type 2 diabetes, although it is no doubt also associated with cardiovascular disease (e.g., Punthakee, Goldenberg, and Katz, 2018).

[5] Data were obtained from both AFFMS I and AFFMS II. As noted in Robson et al., 2021, AFFMS II is reported to present challenges in terms of data quality.

[6] We did not have complete data from 2004 or 2019; however, we did have incomplete data from those years in our overall analysis dataset. We focused on complete data for our analyses relating to career outcomes because these processes are more bound to the calendar and annual cohorts are relevant for these processes. Complete data was not as essential for our analyses of health outcomes, so we used all available data from 2004 to 2019.

have changed over time, we operationalized fitness as AC in inches, time to complete the 1.5-mile run, and the number of push-ups and sit-ups performed during each of those one-minute timed tests. We used these data for our analysis of career outcomes and deployment readiness, as well as health outcomes.[7] Note these quantitative data do not overlap with the COVID-19 pandemic, during which regular administration of the AF-FA was halted, among other effects. We also conducted semi-structured interviews with active duty officers and enlisted personnel to gather insights related to the DAF's culture of fitness.[8]

Career Outcomes and Deployment Readiness

To explore the relationship between component fitness scores and career outcomes, we derived the following variables from the Military Personnel Data System (MilPDS) and other Air Force Personnel Center (AFPC) data sources (see Table 1.1 and Appendix A):

- *Annual retention (officers and enlisted personnel).* We defined *annual retention* as whether an airman remained in the active duty force for the duration of the year.
- *First-term attrition (enlisted personnel).* We defined *first-term attrition* as separation from service that occurred before the end of an airman's first term that was not the result of reenlistment or transfer to the officer corps.[9]
- *First-term promotion (enlisted personnel).* We defined *first-term promotion* as reaching the rank of E-5 within the first four years of service based on date of rank (Asch, Romley, and Totten, 2005). Given that the noncommissioned officer promotion process is merit-based, early promotion to E-5 reveals information about the job-related performance of an airman (AFI 36-2501, 2004).
- *Squadron officer school (SOS) top-third (officers).* We recorded whether airmen who completed SOS in residence graduated within the top-third of their class. This outcome is not directly related to fitness, yet it is one of the top indicators for predicting officer promotion and success (Lim et al., 2014; Military Leadership Diversity Commission, 2011).
- *Ever executive (officers).* We recorded whether airmen ever held an executive officer duty AFSC before meeting their O-4 promotion board. Once again, this outcome is not directly related to fitness, yet it is one of the top indicators for predicting officer promotion and success.
- *Annual deployability (officers and enlisted personnel).* We determined annual deployability by whether an airman was not exempt from deploying for physical reasons.

---

[7] DAF fitness policy (or DAF policy more generally), context, and environment continuously change. For example, our data include a period when the AF underwent significant force reductions, and the data predate the coronavirus disease 2019 (COVID-19) pandemic. Yet, because our data span 15 years, they reveal historically robust relationships of fitness with career outcomes and deployment readiness.

[8] As discussed in Chapter 4, we also asked our interviewees pandemic-related questions.

[9] Because our dataset included only airmen who had completed the AF-FA at least once, our definition of first-term attrition excluded airmen who separated very early in service. We did not assess officer attrition because officer active duty service commitments vary greatly.

Table 1.1. Variable Subgroups, Names, and Availability for Officers and for Enlisted Personnel

Subgroup	Variable	Officer	Enlisted Personnel	Data Source
Career outcome	Annual retention	✓	✓	MilPDS
	First-term attrition	X	✓	MilPDS
	First-term promotion: E-5 in first four years	X	✓	MilPDS
	SOS top-third	✓	X	AFPC
	Ever executive officer (by O-4 board)	✓	X	AFPC
Readiness	Annual deployability	✓	✓	MilPDS

NOTE: ✓ = variable available for subgroup; X = variable not available for subgroup.

Finally, to explore the relationship between fitness and physical readiness for deployment, we identified airmen who could not deploy because of physical deferments that were unlikely to be caused by airman fitness. Therefore, we excluded pregnancy, humanitarian/permissive, and exceptional family member program deferments from our analysis. We retained all other deferments related to an airman's physical disqualifications or limitations.

In addition to the data limitations already noted (some challenges with data quality on AFFMS II and the exclusion of enlisted airmen who separated very early in their service), the lack of granularity and detail for the deployment exemptions presented analytical challenges.

Health Outcomes

To explore the relationship between component fitness scores and health outcomes, we integrated several Defense Health Agency (DHA) databases from the Military Health System Data Repository to create an analytic file of health outcomes. Together, these records provide a picture of all care that airmen received in inpatient and outpatient settings, both at military treatment facilities (MTFs) and outside of MTFs. Each observation in these files represents a medical encounter with patient information, the date of service, and information about the procedures conducted and diagnoses associated with that patient visit. We used data from FY 2004 through FY 2019 because health outcomes relate to processes that unfold more organically over time and are not as calendar bound as are career outcomes.

Information on diagnoses is recorded using International Classification of Diseases (ICD) codes.[10] We used the ICD codes to create indicators of visits in which an airman received a diagnosis for a variety of health conditions. Out of an interest in prioritizing diagnoses with the

---

[10] The ICD coding system is used to categorize both procedures and diagnoses; our analyses focus on the diagnosis codes. In 2016, the ICD system was updated from version 9 (ICD-9) to version 10 (ICD-10) to allow for more specific codes and a more comprehensive coding system that would be more consistent with current medical technology and treatment practices (Cartwright, 2013). As a result, our data include both ICD-9 codes (for encounters before or during FY 2015) and ICD-10 codes (for encounters during or after FY 2016). The ICD-10 system also is set up to allow for future expansions, leading to a more flexible coding system.

highest prevalence and relevance to military fitness, our main analysis focused on the following medical diagnoses and types of injuries, which were selected in consultation with clinical experts and the sponsor:[11]

- hypertension
- other cardiovascular disease, including heart valve disorders, myocarditis/cardiomyopathy, heart disease, heart attacks, cardiac arrest, and aneurisms
- type 2 diabetes
- overuse injuries
- other musculoskeletal conditions, including specific diagnoses for nontraumatic joint or back injuries, traumatic joint or back injuries, fractures, and strains and sprains.

Our data span a period in which both ICD-9 codes and ICD-10 codes were in use.[12] In our analysis, we run separate models for the periods before and after FY 2016 to avoid conflating the effects of the change in coding systems with any actual associations between fitness and health diagnoses. Our primary analyses use ICD-9 codes because they cover a greater number of years.

After identifying the diagnoses, we collapsed the medical encounter records to the person–fiscal year level for our analysis file. Each observation indicates whether an airman received at least one of any of the selected diagnoses in that fiscal year. Then, we linked the health diagnosis data to AF-FA data and AFPC personnel data for our analysis of associations between health conditions and AF-FA scores and other career metrics.[13]

We were able to address some challenges to interpretation, such as the potential for reverse causality (i.e., the possibility that a health diagnosis itself led to a decline in fitness) by using the first year of service (YOS) to predict a new health diagnosis in an airman's second YOS and by further applying survival analysis techniques. An additional challenge inherent to the data relates to the nature of administrative data. Although such data provides an important opportunity for exploring the impact of fitness in the AF, it should be noted that airmen did not leave the sample randomly—less-healthy people were more likely to leave the sample—and we were unable to follow these individuals after their time in service ended.

---

[11] The full list of conditions is quite broad, and it was developed based on a combined review of the literature and discussions with military health experts on common conditions among military populations and common conditions that may be associated with fitness. We considered including metabolic syndrome among the key diagnoses to examine, but existing literature documents that metabolic syndrome is rarely diagnosed using ICD codes and, instead, is diagnosed using other information collected during a physical examination, including blood pressure, cholesterol level, and glucose readings, which we do not observe in the AF data. See, for example, Williams, Oh, and Stahlman, 2018; and Rostami et al., 2019.

[12] We observed a discrete break in the frequency of diagnosed conditions at the beginning of FY 2016 such that diagnoses are more frequent. This change in frequency is consistent with other literature noting the challenges in consistently mapping conditions across the ICD-9 and ICD-10 regimes (e.g., Mainor et al., 2019, and Kusnoor et al., 2020).

[13] We provide further detail on data preparation in Chapter 3.

Culture of Fitness

We also conducted 35 semi-structured telephone interviews with DAF active duty officers and enlisted personnel in a select sample of squadron types of interest to the sponsor (AF's Force Management Policy Directorate [AF/A1P]). The seven (out of 249) squadron types that we selected in consultation with the project sponsor were designed to capture potential variation in fitness levels based on variation in the job characteristics of each squadron type. We contacted 104 airmen in total and had a 34-percent response rate. Table 1.2 shows the number of interviewees from each selected squadron type.

Table 1.2. Semi-Structured Interview Squadron Types

Squadron Type	Number Interviewed
Air refueling	4
Electronic warfare	5
Fighter	5
Force support	6
Missile	4
Space control	6
Special operations	5
Total	35

Overall, we were interested in examining elements related to the DAF's culture of fitness. More specifically, we conducted these interviews to gain insight into airman opinions about and experiences with the AF-FA. We developed the protocol (shown in Appendix C) with feedback from AF/A1P; it has six sections:

- background
- culture of fitness (e.g., "What actions, if any, [have you/has your squadron leadership] taken to promote physical fitness in your unit?")
- barriers to fitness (e.g., "Broadly, what factors do you think contribute to airmen not getting enough exercise?")
- fitness information (e.g., "What additional information would you like to have about the Air Force fitness assessment?")
- current fitness assessment (e.g., "How can the Air Force better use the Air Force fitness assessment to encourage airmen to stay physically fit throughout the year?")
- readiness (e.g., "Do you feel the current Air Force fitness assessment is an accurate or inaccurate measurement of readiness to deploy? Please explain.").

Because we interviewed only a limited number of individuals from seven squadron types, interview results should not be assumed to be representative of all views across the DAF.

Organization of This Report

In the following chapters, we have organized our findings by the concepts, or topics, of focus. In Chapter 2, we describe the results of our analyses of the relationships between AF-FA components and career outcomes and deployment readiness. In Chapter 3, we discuss the results of analyses that examined the relationships between AF-FA components and health outcomes. In Chapter 4, we describe the interview feedback and airman perceptions of the AF-FA and fitness in the DAF more broadly. Finally, in Chapter 5, we discuss the potential implications of the analytical results presented in this report. We also include three appendixes. Appendix A contains more-detailed analyses of the relationships between the AF-FA data and career outcomes. Appendix B provides more-detailed analyses of the relationships between the AF-FA components and health outcomes. Appendix C provides the protocol that we used to guide our interviews.

2. Examining the Relationship Between Airman Fitness and Career Outcomes and Deployment Readiness

In this chapter, we use AF-FA data to address three questions about AF fitness. First, how does the fitness of airmen today compare with the fitness of airmen in the past? This question is motivated in part by data that suggest that many of today's airmen are not physically fit, as reflected by the large percentage classified as "obese" based on BMI alone (Defense Health Agency, 2019). BMI has known limitations and is not a comprehensive measure of fitness (Rothman, 2008; Robson et al., 2022). If airmen were in fact becoming less fit, however, this would have significant implications for military health care costs and readiness.

Second, is fitness associated with first-term attrition, promotion, and other early- and mid-career outcomes? Studies of military populations have shown that poor fitness is a strong risk factor for first-term attrition (National Research Council, 2006). However, the effects of fitness on other early- and mid-career outcomes, such as promotion and selection for competitive duty positions, are less well understood. Fitness could relate to these outcomes for a variety of reasons. For example, airmen who repeatedly fail to meet minimum fitness standards may be subject to negative administrative actions, such as deferred promotion and involuntary separation (AFI 36-2501, 2004). Furthermore, poor fitness may limit an individual's ability to perform demanding occupational tasks and duties required by their career field. Finally, fitness may be a proxy measure for other personality factors, which themselves contribute to career success.

Third, is fitness associated with readiness, as assessed by whether an individual is physically eligible to deploy? Airmen with an unsatisfactory AF-FA composite score are not prohibited from deploying (AFI 36-2905, 2020). However, airmen with low fitness are at increased risk for negative health outcomes, which in turn may disqualify them from deploying.

How Does the Fitness of Airmen Today Compare with the Fitness of Airmen in the Past?

Airmen fitness appears to have improved from FY 2005 to FY 2018. For all airmen (male and female officers and enlisted personnel), the average AC and 1.5-mile run time steadily decreased, and the average number of push-ups and sit-ups increased (Figure 2.1).[14] Specifically, over this 14-year period, these changes represent

- a 3.9-percent decrease in average AC
- a 5.4-percent decrease in the 1.5-mile run time

---

[14] Sample weights were used to adjust for differences in age, gender, and AFSC during different years.

- a 13.5-percent increase in the number of push-ups
- a 14.8-percent increase in the number of sit-ups.

Figure 2.1. Officer and Enlisted Personnel Fitness Scores from FY 2005 to FY 2018, by AF-FA Component and Gender

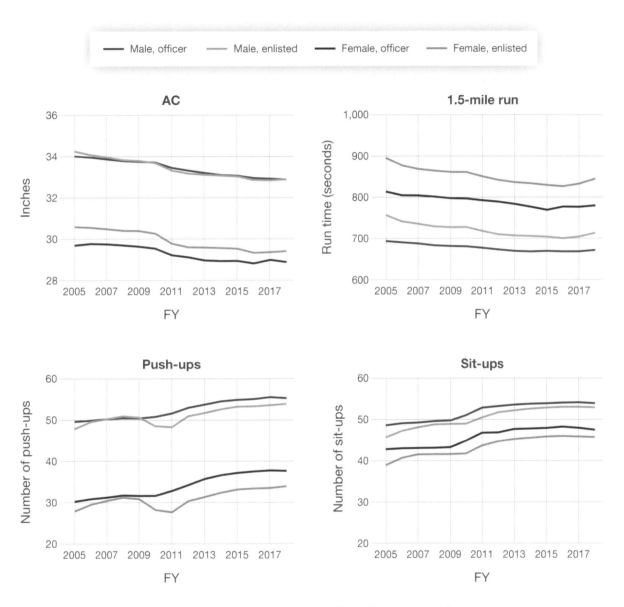

The percentage of component exemptions, excluding those caused by pregnancy or deployment, also varied from FY 2005 to FY 2018. The percentage of AC exemptions decreased, whereas the percentage of 1.5-mile run exemptions increased (Figure 2.2). The percentages of exemptions for push-ups and sit-ups also varied, but they did not systematically change over the 14-year period.

To test whether the improved 1.5-mile run times were an artifact of the increased exemptions (i.e., the least-fit airmen were exempt from the 1.5-mile run in recent years), we repeated the longitudinal analysis for the subset of airmen who were never exempt from the 1.5-mile run. This subset of airmen showed the same annual improvements in aerobic fitness, indicating that the improvement in run times was not an artifact of increased exemptions.

Figure 2.2. Percentages of Officer and Enlisted Personnel Exemptions from FY 2005 to FY 2018, by AF-FA Component and Gender

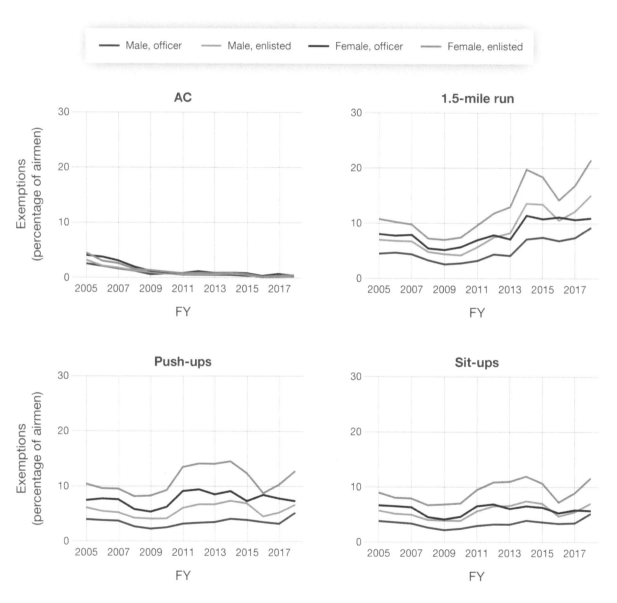

These findings appear at odds with reports that a growing percentage of today's airmen are overweight and obese (Defense Health Agency, 2019). Using height and weight measurements taken during the AF-FA, we computed individual BMIs to classify airmen as "underweight,"

12

"healthy," "overweight," or "obese" per CDC categories.[15] In FY 2005, 64.7 percent of male airmen and 36.9 percent of female airmen could be classified as overweight or obese (Figure 2.3). In FY 2018, the percentage of overweight and obese male airmen remained about the same (63.8 percent) whereas the percentage of overweight and obese female airmen increased to 47.9 percent.

Although these percentages are concerning, BMI does not distinguish between fat mass and other characteristics contributing to an individual's weight, such as muscle and bone. In light of this limitation, researchers have suggested that using BMI alone to estimate military rates of overweight and obese personnel may be inappropriate and may be especially misleading for muscular service members (Meadows et al., 2018). Waist-to-height ratio (WHtR) has been proposed as an alternate measure (Ashwell and Gibson, 2016). We recalculated the percentage of overweight and obese airmen using the AF standard WHtR of 0.5 as the cutoff. The percentage of female airmen who exceed the WHtR cutoff decreased from 22.3 percent in FY 2005 to 14.0 percent in FY 2018, and the percentage of male airmen who exceeded the WHtR cutoff decreased from 37.7 percent to 22.5 percent (Figure 2.3). This improvement contradicts the results found using BMI alone, but it is consistent with the improved AC, aerobic fitness, and muscular fitness of airmen observed from FY 2005 to FY 2018.

---

[15] The CDC defines *BMI* as "a person's weight in kilograms divided by the square of height in meters. A high BMI can be an indicator of high body fatness." The CDC lists four categories based on BMI (CDC, 2021):
- Underweight = < 18.5
- Healthy weight = 18.5–24.9
- Overweight = 25–29.9
- Obesity = 30 or greater.

Figure 2.3. Differences in the Percentages of Officer and Enlisted Personnel Classified as Overweight or Obese from FY 2005 to FY 2018, by Metric and Gender

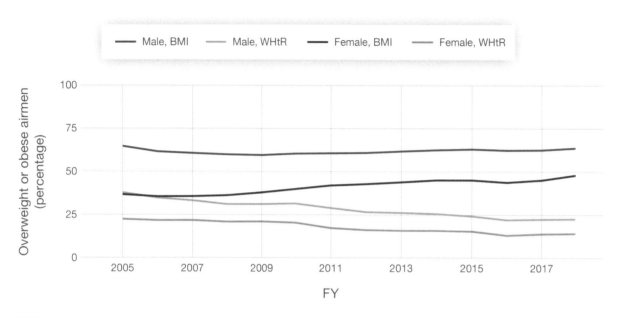

NOTE: This figure shows results for airmen classified as overweight or obese based on BMI ≥ 25 and WHtR ≥ 0.50.

Is Fitness Associated with First-Term Attrition, Promotion, and Other Early- and Mid-Career Outcomes?

To understand the relationship between fitness and career outcomes, we began by modeling annual retention based on AF-FA exemptions and scores.[16] We conducted multivariate logistic regression analyses to account for all AF-FA components and to isolate effects to particular components. Retention rates were lower for airmen who were exempt from at least one component (89.2 percent) versus airmen who were nonexempt from all components (91.8 percent).[17] Curves generated using our statistical model are shown in Figure 2.4. Among airmen who were nonexempt from all components, annual retention in the coming year was further associated with fitness performance in the current year.[18] These effects were greatest for the 1.5-mile run. Being nonexempt from the 1.5-mile run increased the probability of being retained by 1.8 percent, and each unit of improvement in performance among airmen who were

---

[16] Individuals exempt from all AF-FA components (i.e., composite exemptions) were excluded from our analysis. We fitted two models to the remaining data (see Appendix A for details). The first model predicted retention based on exemption status (i.e., whether or not an individual was exempt from each of the four components), and the second predicted retention based on component scores from airmen who were nonexempt from all components. The models controlled for age group, gender, career field, and officer or enlisted rank.

[17] The retention rate values associated with exemption from the aerobic fitness, push-ups, sit-ups, and AC components were 90.0 percent, 88.4 percent, 88.9 percent, and 89.6 percent, respectively.

[18] We treated airmen who completed an alternate aerobic assessment as being exempt.

nonexempt increased the probability further by 1.0 percent.[19] The change appears to be small because retention rates are already very high. However, a 1.8-percent boost in retention reduces the annual separation rate from 10.0 percent to 8.2 percent, or roughly a 20-percent relative reduction in the number of annual separations. This amounts to approximately 5,000 airmen.

Figure 2.4. Relationship Between Retention and Fitness Performance, by AF-FA Component

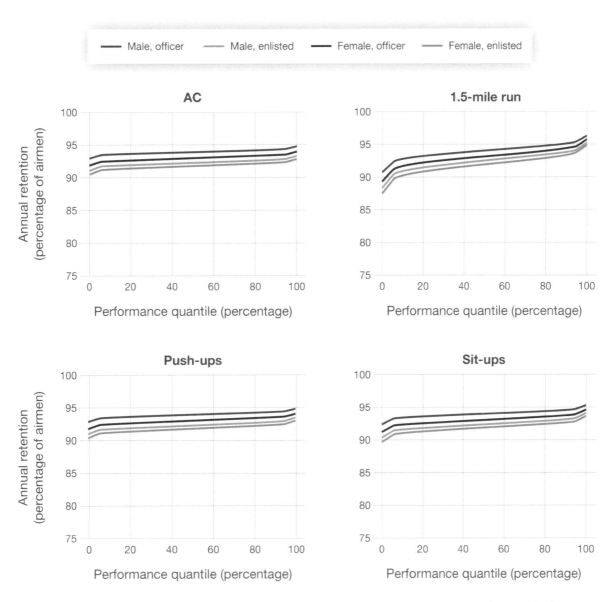

To determine whether fitness was associated with retention across longer time periods, we adopted AF-defined cutoffs to classify low-, moderate-, or high-risk airmen based on their 1.5-mile run time during their first recorded test in their first YOS (AFI 36-2905, 2020). We then

---

[19] *Unit of performance* refers to a one-standard deviation change for a specific fitness component.

calculated retention rates over the first ten YOS separately for the three risk groups. There were notable differences between the groups. Retention rates for high-risk airmen dropped below retention rates for the other cohorts by the second YOS (Figure 2.5). The gap remained during each subsequent YOS and was widest for enlisted personnel at four and six YOS, the typical durations of first-term commitments. The gap was widest for female officers at five YOS, at the time when many would be completing their first active duty service commitment. Retention rates for moderate-risk airmen dropped below retention rates for low-risk airmen by the third YOS and persisted across all subsequent YOS, but the differences were smaller. These annual differences compound over time. The cumulative effect is that far fewer high-risk airmen than moderate- and low-risk airmen were retained through five YOS (50 percent, 69 percent, and 72 percent, respectively) and ten YOS (19 percent, 31 percent, and 38 percent, respectively).

Figure 2.5. Differences in Retention Rate for Officers and Enlisted Personnel, by Initial Fitness Level and Years of Service

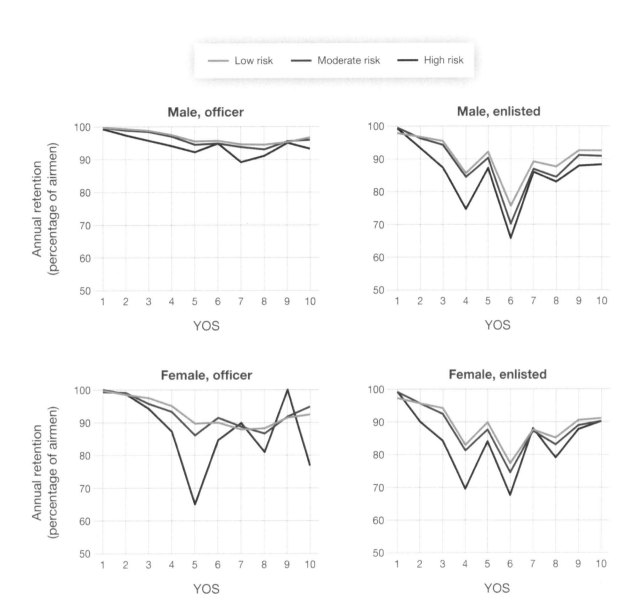

The preceding analysis shows that fitness during the first YOS predicts annual retention through at least the first ten YOS. To examine the association between initial fitness and career success more generally, we modeled the relationship between AF-FA component performance in the first YOS and four future career outcomes:

- Assignment to an executive officer position before meeting an O-4 board
- Graduation from SOS in the top-third of the class
- Early promotion to E-5
- First-term completion for enlisted personnel.

Figure 2.6 shows the marginal change for annual retention and deployability, which applies to all airmen in our sample. It also shows the average increase or decrease in the probabilities of the four career outcomes (i.e., the marginal change) given a one–unit of improvement in each of the AF-FA components.[20] Of the four fitness components, the 1.5-mile run was consistently associated with the largest positive changes in the probabilities of all outcomes (purple bars). For officers, this amounted to 1.4-percent and 4.6-percent increases in the probabilities of being assigned to an executive officer duty position or graduating in the top-third of their SOS class, respectively. For enlisted personnel, this amounted to 1.6-percent increases in the probabilities of completing their first term and receiving an early promotion to E-5.

Push-ups were also consistently associated with positive, but smaller, changes in the probabilities of all outcomes (blue bars). Sit-ups and AC (red and green bars, respectively) were inconsistently associated with small changes (both positive and negative) in the probabilities of the outcomes. The negative effects could be particularly troublesome if they indicated poorer career outcomes for fitter airmen. In the case of AC, the negative effects were not statistically or practically significant (i.e., AC had no real effect on outcomes). In the case of sit-ups, the negative effects were statistically significant in terms of annual deployability and first-term completion by enlisted personnel. However, this unexpected finding warrants two caveats. First, regardless of performance, airmen who completed the sit-ups component were far more likely to be deployable than airmen who were exempt. Second, when treated in isolation, sit-ups were positively associated with annual deployability and first-term completion, as would be expected. The negative associations seen in Figure 2.6 reflect compensation for the fact that airmen who performed well on sit-ups also tended to perform well on other AF-FA components. Therefore, the primary takeaway from this analysis is that completing the sit-ups component and performing well on the other AF-FA components is generally associated with better early-career outcomes.

---

[20] Appendix A contains plots with the probabilities of the four outcomes for different subgroups (male, female, enlisted personnel, and officers) and for different quantile performance scores for the four AF-FA components.

Figure 2.6. Marginal Change in the Probability of an Outcome Given a One-Unit Improvement in Performance for an AF-FA Component

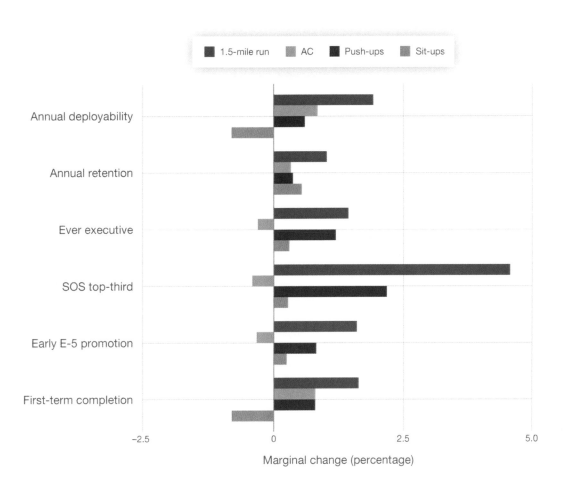

Is Fitness Associated with Deployment Readiness?

To understand the relationship between fitness and readiness, we modeled whether airmen were physically eligible to deploy based on their AF-FA exemptions and scores.[21] The analysis excluded exemptions because of pregnancy. We conducted similar multivariate analyses for all AF-FA components. The probability of being eligible to deploy was lower for airmen who were exempt from at least one component (74.1 percent) versus airmen who were nonexempt from all components (84.3 percent).[22] Figure 2.7 shows the curves generated using our statistical model. Among airmen who were nonexempt from all components, the probability of being eligible to

---

[21] As we did with our analysis of annual retention, we fitted two models to the data (see Appendix A for details). The first predicted whether airmen were eligible to deploy based on their exemption status (i.e., whether or not they were exempt from each of the four AF-FA components), and the second predicted whether airmen who were nonexempt from all components were eligible to deploy based on their AF-FA component scores. The models controlled for age group, gender, career field, and officer or enlisted rank.

[22] The eligibility for deployment values associated with exemption from the aerobic fitness, push-ups, sit-ups, and AC components were 70.0 percent, 74.3 percent, 77.7 percent, and 74.3 percent, respectively.

deploy in the coming year was further associated with fitness performance in the current year. These effects were greatest for the 1.5-mile run. Being nonexempt from the 1.5-mile run increased the probability of being eligible to deploy by 14.8 percent, and each unit of improvement in performance among airmen who were nonexempt increased further the probability of deployment eligibility by 1.9 percent.

Figure 2.7. Relationship Between Deployability and Fitness Performance, by AF-FA Component and Gender

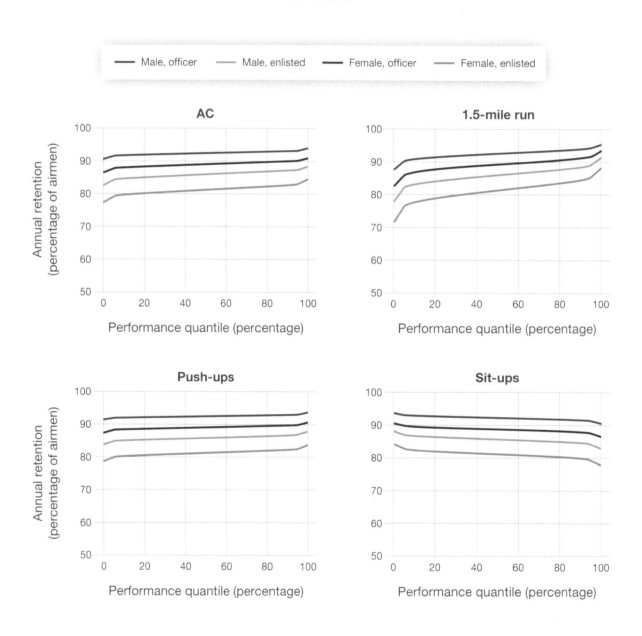

20

Summary

The purpose of the AF physical fitness program is to motivate airmen to participate in year-long physical conditioning to promote their health, well-being, and readiness. The AF-FA provides an annual snapshot of an airman's body composition, aerobic fitness, and muscular fitness. The data captured during the AF-FA provide an opportunity to examine changes over time in airman fitness and to explore relationships between fitness and annual and career outcomes.

The analyses reported in this chapter support several conclusions:

- Although the average BMI of airmen has increased from FY 2005 to FY 2018, WHtR has decreased. Additionally, average aerobic and muscular fitness levels have increased. Together, these results suggest that airman fitness has actually improved over time.
- Multiple AF-FA components are positively associated with annual retention and physical eligibility for deployment, and the strength of association is greatest for aerobic fitness, as assessed by the 1.5-mile run.
- Likewise, multiple AF-FA components are positively associated with early- and mid-career outcomes, and the strength of association is again greatest for aerobic fitness.
- The associations span multiple years: Fitness in the very first YOS predicted annual and career outcomes over the first ten YOS.

A limitation of these analyses is that they do not determine the nature of the relationship between fitness and annual and career outcomes. The relationship could be causal. For example, fitter airmen may experience fewer negative health outcomes, allowing them to remain physically eligible for deployment. The relationship could also be correlational. For example, fitness may be associated with other personality factors, which themselves contribute to career success. The fitness data alone do not permit us to make a distinction between these possibilities. Nevertheless, the analyses illustrate the association between fitness and outcomes that the DAF seeks to influence, and they raise the possibility of a meaningful relationship between airman fitness, readiness, and career success.

3. Examining the Relationship Between Airman Fitness and Health Outcomes

As noted in Chapter 1, there is well-established literature showing that physical fitness is linked to general good health and well-being, although this linkage has yet to be fully explored in a young and healthy population, such as the AF's active duty component. A basic level of physical health is beneficial for the performance of any work, including AF jobs performed both at home station and on deployment. Therefore, we examined AF-FA data to determine the relationship between airman fitness and health outcomes. The results of our analyses may provide the DAF with the means to set evidence-based fitness standards going forward.

We examined the following topics:

- the prevalence of various diagnoses received by airmen over time. This analysis provided a baseline for health and injury diagnoses in our population while adding to the consideration of airman health over time, as described in Chapter 2.
- the relevance of fitness, as assessed by the AF-FA, to health and injury diagnoses as determined by

    - the immediate influence of fitness on airman health in the subsequent year
    - whether an airman's fitness category influenced their short-term health outcomes
    - whether airman fitness *as it varied over time* influenced health and injury diagnoses (continuing our examination of the effects of fitness on health over time)

- whether exemptions had a relationship to health outcomes. Some categories of exemption (e.g., medical, commander's exemption) could potentially serve as early warnings of later health concerns.

Prevalence of Diagnoses Among Airmen

Before examining the relationship between airman fitness and health outcomes, we first sought to understand the frequency of diagnoses among airmen. We used ICD codes to create indicators for visits that had one of the diagnoses shown in Table 3.1, which we selected in consultation with clinical experts.

Table 3.1. Health Conditions Included in Our Analysis

Condition Category	Diagnosis
Cardiovascular conditions	• Hypertension • Other cardiovascular disease, including heart valve disorders, myocarditis/cardiomyopathy, heart disease, heart attacks, cardiac arrest, aneurisms
Diabetes	• Diabetes
Overuse injuries	• Overuse injuries
Other musculoskeletal conditions	• Nontraumatic joint or back injuries • Traumatic joint or back injuries • Fractures • Strains and sprains

We examined two types of diagnoses in our detailed analyses: (1) health diagnoses (cardiovascular conditions and diabetes) and (2) injury diagnoses (overuse injuries and other musculoskeletal conditions). We considered these diagnoses separately (see Table 3.1). Because the clinical classifications software (CCS) does not have a specific category for overuse injuries,[23] we used existing literature as the primary source for determining which ICD codes should be used to identify overuse injuries (Hauret et al., 2010; Hauschild et al., 2017; Schuh-Renner et al., 2019). Unless otherwise noted, the results presented in this chapter are based on our analysis of DHA data linked to AFPC and AF-FA data from FY 2004 to FY 2015.

Even in our relatively young and healthy sample population, various diagnoses are not uncommon. Figure 3.1 shows the trends in the three specific health diagnoses in our set of analyzed health conditions. Overall, the rates were extremely stable from FY 2004 to FY 2015, although there has been an increase in the prevalence of diagnosed cardiovascular conditions since then, reaching over 10 percent by 2019. This trend is likely due to changes in coding methodology under ICD-10, rather than an increase in the prevalence of cardiovascular diagnoses among airmen. Diabetes diagnoses were less frequent: Less than 1 percent of both female and male airmen received a new diabetes diagnosis each fiscal year.[24]

---

[23] We used the CCS to group specific ICD codes into the health condition categories of interest and refined their classification based on reviews of existing medical and health services literature and discussion with clinical experts.

[24] We considered a new diagnosis to be one that was not recorded in a prior fiscal year during the period of time in which we were able to observe the airman's medical records in the analytic file. Note, however, that we only observed TRICARE records, so if the airman received care outside of the TRICARE system, it would not be observed in our data.

Figure 3.1. Frequency of Specific Health Diagnoses Among Airmen over Time, by Gender

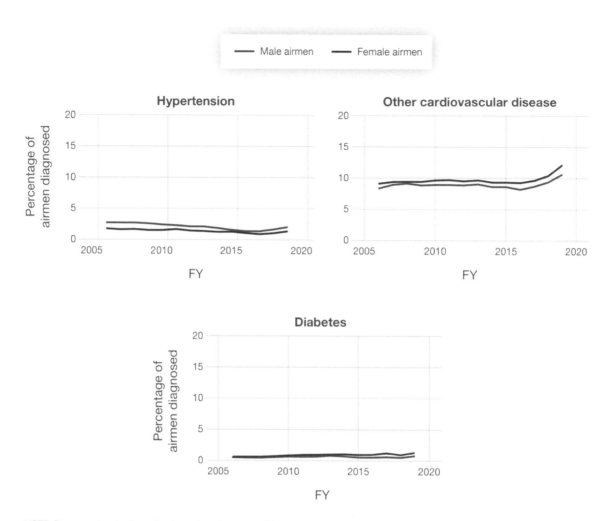

As shown in Figure 3.2, overuse injuries were among the most common types of injury diagnosis observed. Approximately 18–19 percent of female airmen and 16–17 percent of male airmen were diagnosed with a new overuse injury each year from FY 2004 to FY 2015, although, again, the frequency increased sharply with the introduction of ICD-10 in 2016, increasing to more than 20 percent for female airmen and more than 18 percent for male airmen. Between 15–16 percent of female airmen and 13–14 percent of male airmen received a new other musculoskeletal injury diagnosis from FY 2004 to FY 2015, although there was a slight decline in the frequency of other musculoskeletal injury diagnoses over this time frame. The decline starts in 2016, falling to 10–11 percent for both female and male airmen.

Interestingly, the rate of diagnosis for both overuse injuries and other musculoskeletal conditions was higher among female airmen, although the overall number of diagnoses was much higher among male airmen due to the fact that they made up the majority (approximately 80 percent) of the sample population.

Figure 3.2. Frequency of Specific Injury Diagnoses Among Airmen over Time, by Gender

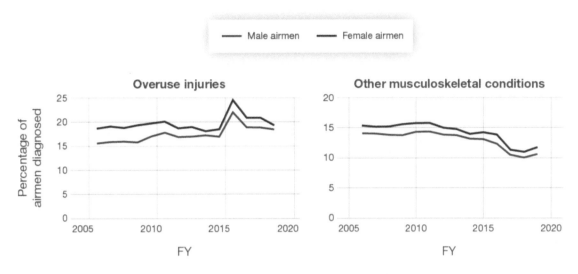

NOTE: Diagnoses trends shown for airmen in their second YOS are consistent with the years of outcomes examined in our analysis.

The Relationship Between Airman Fitness and Health and Injury Diagnoses

Next, we examined the association between fitness and medical diagnoses. Specifically, these analyses address whether the AF-FA components (1.5-mile run, AC, push-ups, and sit-ups) are associated with the most-prevalent health and injury diagnoses among airmen, which are, according to clinical experts and the literature, also the most relevant to fitness. The following sections describe our analytical approach, statistical analyses, and findings.

Analytical Approach

We used multiple types of analyses to examine how fitness might be related to health and injury diagnoses and to answer different questions.[25] Although each analysis offers a slightly different way to explore such relationships, the results generally support the same conclusions. Observed correlations, however, do not necessarily indicate a causal relationship. Even so, these analyses demonstrate how AF-FA components might be used to predict physical health and injury diagnoses and, by extension, health outcomes. These indicators may help identify airmen who could be at increased risk of developing adverse physical health conditions in the future.

First, we used multivariate logistic regression analyses to examine how well airman fitness in the first YOS predicted the occurrence of a *new* health or injury diagnosis in their second YOS. By predicting future diagnoses, this analysis helps avoid concerns of reverse causality (i.e., that

---

[25] Details on the different types of analyses that we conducted and the results of the different models are presented in Appendix B.

the health diagnosis itself led to a decline in fitness).[26] These analyses establish an understanding of the relevance of the AF-FA, even for airmen early in their careers, when the risk of negative health events is at its lowest.

Although these analyses explore whether fitness scores from an airman's first year can be used to predict their risk of diagnosis in the following year, fitness levels change over time and many airmen may reenlist and serve for more than one term. To address these points, we conducted survival analysis.[27]

Specifically, we explored the hazard ratios for adverse health outcomes resulting from different fitness levels by using a Cox proportional-hazards model to estimate the hazard ratios of receiving a health or injury diagnosis based on an airmen's current fitness level. The term *hazard* refers to the rate of occurrence (i.e., percentage of airmen having a specific health outcome). We have chosen not to use the term *risk* to describe rate of occurrence, as is commonly used, to avoid confusion with the fitness categories (e.g., low, moderate, and high risk) that we use in our analysis. Thus, *hazard ratio* refers to the amount of increased likelihood of diagnosis for airmen who are in the moderate- or high-risk categories compared with airmen in the low-risk category for a specific AF-FA component.

Variables Used in Our Models

Our analyses considered AF-FA component scores and other airman characteristics that could be related to health outcomes to understand the role that the AF-FA components played while controlling for other relevant characteristics.[28] Table 3.2 shows the full set of variables that we used in our health outcome analyses.

Table 3.2. Variables Used in Health Outcome Analyses

AF-FA Component	Control	Diagnosis (Type)
AC	Prior diagnosis (post-BMT)	Diabetes (health)
1.5-mile run	Gender	Hypertension (health)
Push-ups	Age group	Other cardiovascular disease (health)
Sit-ups	Officer/enlisted	Overuse injuries (injury)
	Ever deployed	Other musculoskeletal conditions (injury)
	Race/ethnicity	

NOTE: BMT = Basic Military Training.

---

[26] Our focus on new diagnoses also helped to address concerns of whether airmen with ongoing conditions may have lower performance on the AF-FA.

[27] Survival analysis is a common approach in health-related fields in which the probability of an event is modeled, prototypically, as survival or death. However, in the current context, survival means an airman does not receive one of the specific diagnoses that we include in our analysis.

[28] The purpose of controlling for these other characteristics was to ensure that differences in health outcomes for airmen with different fitness levels was not due to other known factors that could influence health, such as age or gender. Multivariate logistic regressions also accounted for airmen's height, weight, and YOS and examined only new diagnoses, so prior diagnoses were irrelevant.

Relationship Between Fitness and Health Diagnoses

Does Initial Fitness Predict the Odds of Health Diagnoses in Airmen's Second Year of Service?

In our initial analyses, we used multivariate logistic regression to explore the relationship between airmen's first YOS fitness scores and the likelihood of airmen receiving a new health diagnosis in the following year. In general, these analyses found that having lower fitness was associated with a higher probability of receiving a health diagnosis. (Odds ratios are shown in Table 3.3. An odds ratio greater than 1 indicates a higher probability of diagnosis while an odds ratio of less than 1 indicates a lower probability.) In terms of specific AF-FA components, a higher AC and run time were associated with a higher probability of a diagnosis for hypertension in the second YOS (in both cases, there is about a 5-percent increase in the likelihood of a diagnosis). One exception was the relationship between sit-ups and other cardiovascular disease diagnoses. Contrary to the expected direction, performing a higher number of sit-ups in the first YOS was associated with a small, yet still significant, increased likelihood of other cardiovascular disease diagnoses. This was also true for the relationship between push-ups and hypertension; however, the effect sizes for these results were quite small.

Table 3.3. Estimated Odds Ratios for First-Year Observed Fitness Scores on New Health Diagnoses in the Second Year of Service

	Health Diagnosis		
AF-FA Component	**Hypertension**	**Other Cardiovascular Disease**	**Diabetes**
AC	1.044*	0.999	0.985
	(0.007)	(0.003)	(0.016)
1.5-mile run	1.054*	1.041*	1.040
	(0.005)	(0.003)	(0.010)
Sit-ups	1.001	1.003*	0.996
	(0.002)	(0.001)	(0.004)
Push-ups	1.006*	1.001	0.993
	(0.001)	(0.001)	(0.003)

NOTE: Estimates for run times are scaled to minutes, AC is measured in inches, and sit-ups and push-ups in the number completed within one minute. Standard errors are shown in parentheses.
*$p < 0.05$.

What Is the Probability of Diagnosis Within the First Four Years of Service Based on an Airman's Initial Fitness Category?

Using survival analyses (for details, see Appendix B), we estimated the expected incidence of each health diagnosis based on an airman's baseline (first-year) fitness category. These results, presented in Figure 3.3, show that airmen in the high-risk category are more likely to receive a health diagnosis within their first four YOS compared with airmen in either the moderate- or low-risk category for AC. For example, airmen in the low-risk category for AC in their first year have only a 5-percent likelihood of receiving a hypertension diagnosis in their first four YOS. In contrast, airmen in the high-risk category for AC have a 24-percent likelihood of a hypertension diagnosis. Figure 3.3 also shows that results for other AF-FA components are generally not as dramatic as these AC results.

Figure 3.3. Airman Risk of a Health Diagnosis Within First Four Years of Service, by Fitness Category

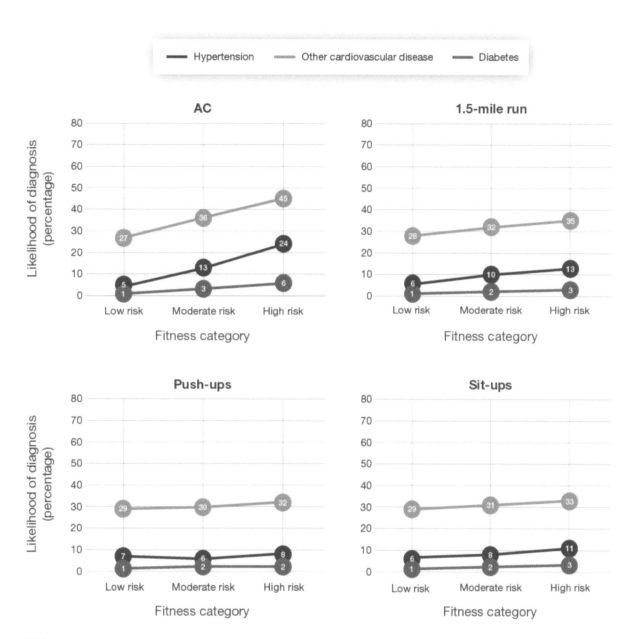

NOTE: For the survival analyses, we adapted low-, moderate-, and high-risk fitness categories based on the AF-FA scoring system (AFI 36-2905, 2020) for each of the four AF-FA components. Fitness scores for AC and cardiorespiratory endurance (i.e., the 1.5-mile run) are determined by AF standards, which we used to generate cutoffs for approximately equivalent fitness categories for push-ups and sit-ups. For AC, standards vary by gender, and for the 1.5-mile run, standards vary by gender and age. Values shown are the estimated percentages of airmen with first-year fitness scores in each of the designated fitness categories who would likely receive each diagnosis within their first four YOS.

What Is the Relative Likelihood of Receiving a Health Diagnosis Based on an Airman's Most-Recent Fitness Scores?

Expanding beyond an airman's first YOS, we conducted analyses that update fitness scores each year to reflect current fitness levels over the course of an airman's career. Specifically, we used a Cox proportional-hazards model to estimate the hazard ratios for moderate- and high-risk airmen relative to low-risk airmen.[29] An estimated hazard ratio of 1 means that airmen in an elevated-risk fitness category have the same likelihood of receiving a health diagnosis relative to airmen in the low-risk category. Looking at the top-left cells in Table 3.4, these results show that, when controlling for fitness levels on all other components and demographic factors, airmen in the moderate- or high-risk fitness categories for AC have an estimated 1.86 times and 3.53 times respectively higher likelihood of a diabetes diagnosis than airmen in the low-risk fitness category for AC. Furthermore, airmen in the high-risk AC category are 3.25 times more likely to receive a hypertension diagnosis compared with those in the low-risk AC category. The hazard ratios are positive but smaller for the 1.5-mile run and sit-ups suggesting that running faster and performing more sit-ups is associated with a lower likelihood of diagnosis. Being in either the moderate- or high-risk category for push-ups did not consistently increase the likelihood of receiving a health diagnosis, given the small hazard ratios.

Table 3.4. Estimated Hazard Ratios for Health Diagnoses, by AF-FA Component and Fitness Category

AF-FA Component	Fitness Category	Health Diagnosis		
		Hypertension	Other Cardiovascular Disease	Diabetes
AC	Moderate risk	2.01*	1.34*	1.86*
	High risk	3.25*	1.74*	3.53*
1.5-mile run	Moderate risk	1.35*	1.12*	1.40*
	High risk	1.85*	1.42*	1.94*
Push-ups	Moderate risk	0.98	1.03*	1.04
	High risk	1.00	1.05*	1.02
Sit-ups	Moderate risk	1.16*	1.05*	1.20*
	High risk	1.30*	1.08*	1.38*

NOTE: For each of the four fitness components, we adapted low-, moderate-, or high-risk fitness categories based on the AF-FA scoring system (AFI 36-2905, 2020). Values shown are estimated hazard ratios (i.e., *greater* likelihood of diagnosis when the ratio is greater than 1) for airmen of receiving each diagnosis over the course of their careers if their fitness levels fall within the moderate- or high-risk fitness categories (relative to airmen in the low-risk fitness category). Hazard ratios are estimated controlling for all fitness categories and airman demographics. *$p < 0.05$.

Relationship Between Fitness and Injury Diagnoses

Adopting the same strategy that we used to evaluate health diagnoses, we evaluated the relationship between airman fitness and injury diagnoses. Unlike the relationship between fitness

---

[29] In the event that an airman's AF-FA component score was missing or exempt, the component score was not updated, and the previous score remained until a new AF-FA was performed.

and health diagnoses, the pattern of relationships between fitness and injury diagnoses depends on the type of analysis. For example, when using survival models, we found that a higher AC was associated with increased likelihood of an injury. However, the direction of the relationship was reversed when using logistic regression. That is, airmen who had lower ACs in their first YOS were more likely to receive an overuse injury diagnosis in their second YOS.

Although further research is needed to disentangle the inconsistent relationships that we observed between these two types of analyses, one plausible explanation is that airmen with high ACs may have less risk over a relatively shorter period of time because of physical inactivity, but that likelihood of overuse injury may increase over longer periods of time (e.g., multiple years) as airmen must engage in some amount of physical activity to meet AF-FA requirements. The higher rate of overuse injuries among a more fit population may perhaps be the result of higher levels of physical activity or, in some cases, overtraining (Hoffman, Church, and Hoffman, 2016; Wheeler and Wenke, 2018).

Does Initial Fitness Predict Injury Diagnoses in an Airman's Second Year of Service?

Of the four AF-FA components, only sit-ups were consistently related to the likelihood of an injury diagnosis (see Table 3.5). However, the relationships indicated that better sit-up performance was associated with a slightly higher probability of an overuse or other musculoskeletal injury. The 1.5-mile run was not associated with the likelihood of an injury in the second YOS. AC and push-ups were also not consistently related to injury diagnoses. Specifically, AC was negatively related to the likelihood of an overuse injury but not of other musculoskeletal conditions. Sit-ups were positively related to the likelihood of a diagnosis for both overuse injury and other musculoskeletal conditions. This general pattern of results suggests that there may be some likelihood of an injury for airmen who demonstrate higher levels of fitness on their initial AF-FA (i.e., having a low AC and performing a high number of sit-ups).

Table 3.5. Estimated Odds Ratios of First-Year Observed Fitness on New Injury Diagnoses in the Second Year

AF-FA Component	Overuse Injuries	Other Musculoskeletal Conditions
AC	0.990*	1.004
	(0.002)	(0.002)
1.5-mile run	1.008*	1.009*
	(0.002)	(0.002)
Sit-ups	1.002*	1.002*
	(0.001)	(0.001)
Push-ups	1.001	0.994
	(0.000)	(0.001)

NOTE: Estimates for run times are scaled to minutes, AC is measured in inches, and sit-ups and push-ups in the number of each performed within one minute. Standard errors are shown in parentheses. * $p < 0.05$

What Is the Probability of Receiving an Injury Diagnosis Within the First Four Years of Service Based on an Airman's Initial Fitness Category?

For each AF-FA component, the relationships suggest that having lower fitness during the first year is a risk factor for an overuse or musculoskeletal injury, as shown in Figure 3.4. Airmen in the high-risk category for AC had a 71-percent probability of receiving an injury diagnosis in their first four YOS compared with a 56-percent probability for airmen with a low-risk AC. The direction of the relationships between the other fitness components and injuries was the same, although the increases in probability of injury for airmen in the moderate- and high-risk categories were relatively small. At most, the likelihood of an injury in the first four YOS increased by only 5 percent for airmen in the high-risk category compared with airmen in the low-risk category. For example, airmen in the high-risk category for the 1.5-mile run had a 61-percent probability of receiving an injury diagnosis compared with a 57-percent probability for airmen in the low-risk category.

Figure 3.4. Risk of an Injury Diagnosis Within an Airman's First Four Years of Service

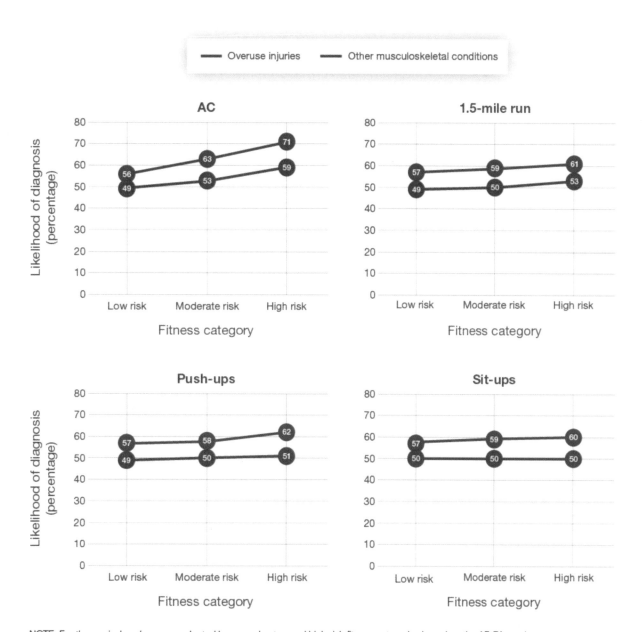

NOTE: For the survival analyses, we adapted low-, moderate-, and high-risk fitness categories based on the AF-FA scoring system (AFI 36-2905, 2020) for each of the four AF-FA components. Fitness scores for AC and cardiorespiratory endurance (i.e., the 1.5-mile run) are determined by AF standards, which we used to generate cutoffs for approximately equivalent fitness categories for push-ups and sit-ups. For AC, standards vary by gender, and for the 1.5-mile run, standards vary by gender and age. Values shown are the estimated percentages of airmen with first-year fitness scores in each of the designated categories who would likely receive each diagnosis within their first four YOS.

What Is the Likelihood of an Injury Diagnosis Based on an Airman's Most-Recent Fitness Scores?

The hazard ratios for airmen in the moderate- and high-risk fitness categories relative to airmen in the low-risk category for each AF-FA component model are provided for all airmen combined in Table 3.6. We provide the hazard ratios for all airmen by gender and by racial/ethnic group separately in Appendix B.[30]

Our results indicate that relative to airmen in the low-risk category, airmen in moderate- and high-risk categories (based on their most-recent AC score) have, respectively, a 19-percent and a 48-percent higher likelihood of receiving an overuse injury diagnosis and similar increases in risk for other musculoskeletal conditions. Airmen in the moderate- or high-risk run time category had a 4-percent and 25-percent increased likelihood of overuse injuries, respectively and, if they are in the high-risk category, a 20-percent increased likelihood for other musculoskeletal injuries. Individuals in moderate or high-risk categories for push-ups have a slightly higher chance of overuse but no increased likelihood of other musculoskeletal injuries for those in the moderate-risk category. Individuals in moderate or high-risk categories for sit-ups did not have elevated likelihood of overuse diagnoses and showed a slightly decreased likelihood of other musculoskeletal injuries.

Table 3.6. Estimated Hazard Ratios for Injury Diagnoses, by Fitness Category and Diagnosis Type

		Injury Diagnosis	
AF-FA Component	Fitness Category	Overuse Injuries	Other Musculoskeletal Conditions
AC	Moderate Risk	1.19*	1.22*
	High Risk	1.48*	1.49*
1.5-mile run	Moderate Risk	1.04*	1.01
	High Risk	1.25*	1.20*
Push-ups	Moderate Risk	1.03*	1.00
	High Risk	1.08*	1.03*
Sit-ups	Moderate Risk	0.99	0.97*
	High Risk	1.00	0.97*

NOTE: For each of the four fitness components, we adapted low-, moderate-, or high-risk fitness categories based on the AF-FA scoring system (AFI 36-2905, 2020). Values shown are estimated hazard ratios (i.e., *greater* likelihood of diagnosis when the ratio is greater than 1) for airmen of receiving each diagnosis over the course of their careers if their fitness levels fall within the moderate- or high-risk fitness categories (relative to airmen in the low-risk fitness category). Hazard ratios are estimated controlling for all fitness categories and airman demographics. *$p < 0.05$

Exemptions

As we discussed in Chapter 2, airmen may receive an exemption from the AF-FA for a variety of reasons, including pregnancy, deployment, and certain medical conditions. Because

---

[30] These results show that estimated hazard ratios can sometimes differ between different racial/ethnic groups and between genders. This suggests that the fitness risk categories have differential predictive power for health outcomes by gender and race/ethnicity, and a one-size-fits-all fitness standard may not serve all airmen well.

AF-FA scores are not available when airmen receive an exemption, we modeled the relationship between exemptions and health outcomes separately. In this set of analyses, we examined the relationship between exemptions and future diagnoses. Exemptions for reasons other than deployment or pregnancy may, in themselves, be seen as potential indicators of poor health that has not (yet) risen to the level of a diagnosis. Moreover, examining exemptions allows us to include airmen who would otherwise not be included in the analysis. We estimated similar multivariate models as in our logistic regression analyses but included indicators for having exemptions for the various components rather than the AF-FA scores. We excluded pregnancy and deployment exemptions from this analysis.

As shown in Figure 3.5, having an exemption for AC in the first year is associated with a lower likelihood of a new cardiovascular disease diagnosis in the second year, while having an exemption for the 1.5-mile run or sit-ups in the first year is associated with a higher likelihood of having a new cardiovascular disease diagnosis in the second year (the relationship between fitness and the push-ups exemption was not significant for this diagnosis). Finally, having an exemption on the 1.5-mile run or sit-ups component also increased the likelihood of an airman receiving new diagnoses for hypertension and diabetes in the second year (the relationships between fitness and the push-ups exemption for these diagnoses were not significant). Except for AC, the likelihood of receiving a health diagnosis increases with AF-FA component exemptions.

Figure 3.5. Change in the Probability of Health Diagnoses Following an Exemption, by AF-FA Component

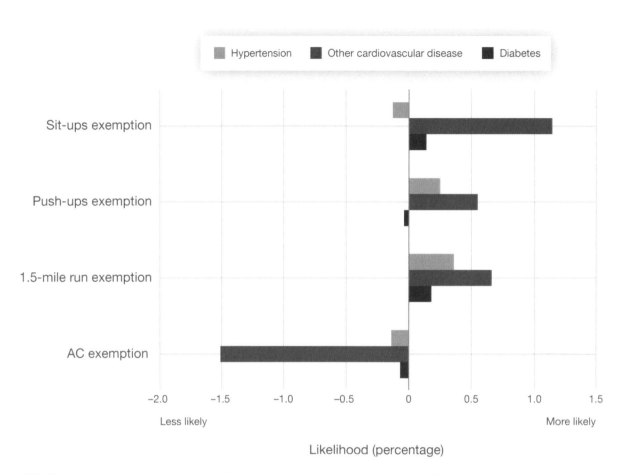

NOTE: The figure shows the relationship between fitness exemptions in the second year observed with new diagnoses in the third year observed.

The relationships between each AF-FA component exemption and injury diagnoses are presented in Figure 3.6. AC exemptions are strongly predictive of future overuse injury diagnoses, while exemptions for the other AF-FA components are all negatively associated with the probability of a new overuse injury diagnosis in the second year. Exemptions for the 1.5-mile run were also negatively associated with the probability of a new diagnosis for other musculoskeletal conditions. There were no relationships between AC, push-ups, or sit-ups exemptions and other musculoskeletal diagnoses. Although injuries are complex diagnoses, with many potential causes, the relationships suggest that airmen with muscular fitness exemptions may be slightly more likely to receive injury diagnoses.

Figure 3.6. Change in the Probability of Injury Diagnoses Following an Exemption

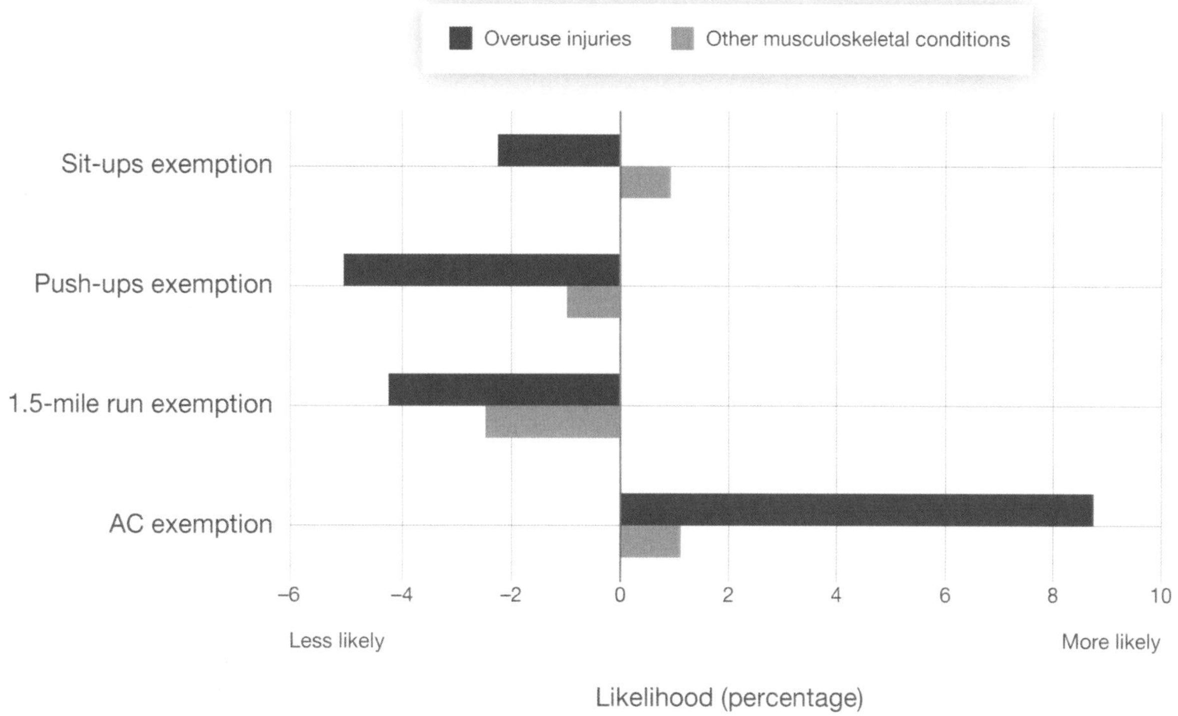

Because the reasons for exemption may vary, there could be many factors that explain the strength and direction of the relationship between exemptions and future health outcomes. For example, exemptions because of medical reasons may signal a greater likelihood of future diagnoses for a generally less healthy population, but it may be unrelated to airman fitness. Nevertheless, these analyses demonstrate that the presence of an exemption in an airman's first year is generally associated with an increased likelihood of receiving future health and injury diagnoses.

Overall Airman Fitness and Health Outcomes

The previous set of analyses assesses the relationships between each AF-FA component, exemptions, and the likelihood of receiving a diagnosis, but this analysis does not address whether overall airman fitness can predict the future health of the force. To examine this question, we ranked all AF-FA component scores from best to worst, estimated the likelihood of having a new hypertension diagnosis for an airman who scored in the top 10th percentile (i.e., best performance) on each AF-FA component, and compared the estimated probability of a future hypertension diagnosis with an airman who scored in the 90th percentile (i.e., worst performance) on each AF-FA component.

The results, presented in Figure 3.7, suggest that a male airman in the top 10th percentile on each component has a 1.8-percent probability of receiving a hypertension diagnosis in the following year, compared with a 2.3-percent probability for a male airman in the 90th percentile on each component score. This difference represents a 27-percent change in the likelihood of a hypertension diagnosis. Female airmen performing in the top 10th percentile have a 1.1-percent probability of receiving a hypertension diagnosis compared with a 1.5-percent probability for female airmen at the 90th percentile—a change of 36 percent.

For another perspective, consider the effect of an incremental change in fitness for just one component in the AF-FA. There are approximately 260,000 male airmen and 60,000 female airmen observed each year in the data between FY 2004 and 2015. Suppose the entire population had the median run time score. At this rate, our estimates suggest that approximately 5,460 male airmen and 750 female airmen would receive a new diagnosis for a hypertension in the following year. If run times for all airmen slowed to the 75th percentile, this would be associated with an increase of 270 additional cardiovascular diagnoses. While the relative magnitude of this change is small, it is important to keep in mind that this analysis represents a point in time analysis showing the effect on cardiovascular diagnoses over just one year in an airman's career.

Figure 3.7. Predicted Likelihood of Hypertension Diagnosis for Airmen at the 10th and 90th Percentiles of AF-FA Component Scores, by Gender

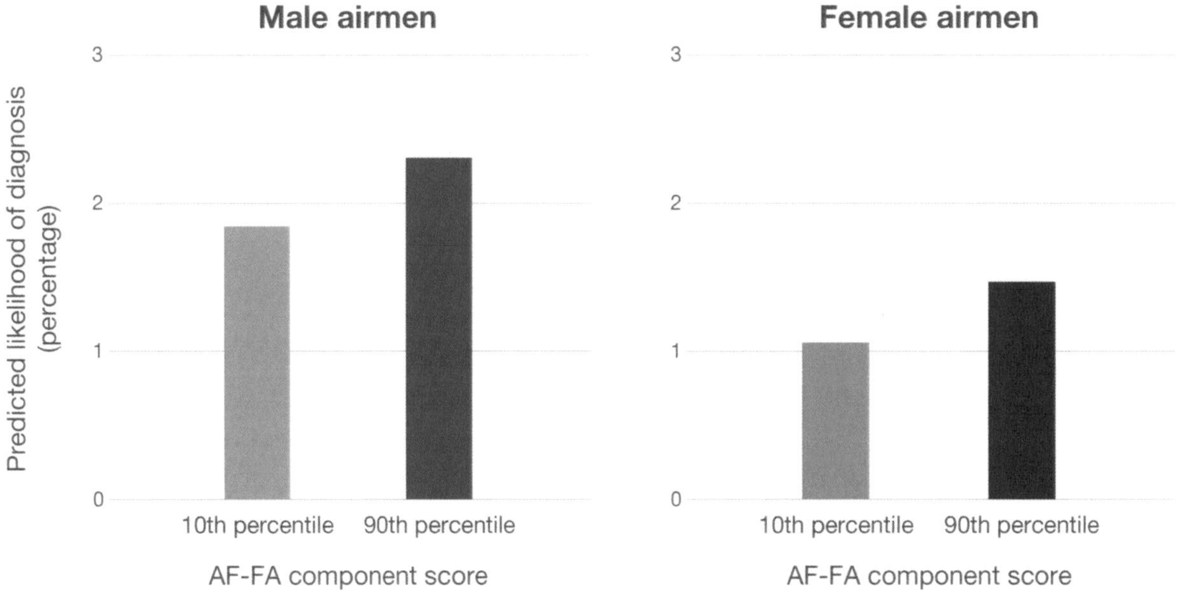

NOTE: Figure shows estimated probability of a new hypertension diagnosis while holding AF-FA component scores constant at the 10th and 90th percentiles, respectively.

If there are incremental changes in airman scores over time, their effects could accumulate and compound because new diagnoses require continuous management. As we noted in Chapter 2, scores for several AF-FA components have improved over the past few years, suggesting that this scenario may be unlikely. However, these results present a picture of potential risks if airmen do not maintain their fitness.

Summary

Four different analytical approaches most clearly support the inclusion of the AC and 1.5-mile run scores as indicators of health risk. The analytical results also support the following conclusions:

- Performance on the AF-FA components is a positive indicator of airman health.
- The relationships with health outcomes were generally strongest for AC, followed by the 1.5-mile run.
- The relationship between the sit-ups and push-ups components and health outcomes was more mixed.
- The relationships between AC and musculoskeletal injuries were inconsistent and require further research to disentangle possible confounding factors.
- The relationship between the 1.5-mile run, push-ups, sit-ups components and injury diagnoses was also mixed, with some evidence suggesting that fitter airmen may be at greater risk of injury.

We summarize these findings below in Table 3.7. Generally, our analyses also support the contention that fitness risk levels, as defined by AFI 36-2905, 2020, do distinguish between airmen's likelihood of various negative health outcomes.

Table 3.7. Summary of AF-FA Component Relationships with Health Outcomes

AF-FA Component	Health Diagnoses			Injury Diagnoses	
	Hypertension	Other Cardiovascular	Diabetes	Overuse Injuries	Other Musculoskeletal Conditions
AC	Hazard increases substantially with higher AC	Hazard increases with higher AC	Hazard increases substantially with higher AC	Some mixed results but general pattern suggested that hazard increases with higher AC	
1.5-mile run	Hazard increases with slower run times	Hazard increases with slower run times	Hazard increases with slower run times	Mixed results; general patterns suggest a slight increase in hazard with faster run times	
Sit-ups	Hazard increases with fewer sit-ups	Mixed results	Hazard increases with fewer sit-ups	Mixed results; strength of any relationship to injuries is weak	
Push-ups	Hazard unaffected	Hazard slightly increases with fewer push-ups	Hazard unaffected	Mixed results; strength of any relationship to injuries is weak	

NOTE: As a reminder, *hazard* refers to the likelihood of receiving a specific diagnosis.

It is important to note that our analyses controlled for only a subset of factors that could potentially be correlated with health and injury diagnoses. For example, other health characteristics, such as use of alcohol and tobacco, family medical history, and results from other health-screening measures (e.g., glucose or cholesterol), could also be important factors that would affect airman risk of developing health conditions. Other factors, such as job type, could be an important factor for overuse injuries or other musculoskeletal conditions, although exploration of that aspect delves into consideration of Tier 2 (job-related) standards, which is beyond the scope of this analysis.[31] As more-complete data become available on these factors, future work should incorporate them to develop a more comprehensive risk assessment model.

Finally, these analyses provide a preliminary picture on the strength and level of association between AF-FA components and health outcomes among all airmen. Although we provide exploratory analyses by gender (see Appendix B), future work should also be conducted to more carefully explore the extent to which the relationship between fitness components, other unobserved factors, and health outcomes varies by gender and race/ethnicity. These analyses, while advancing the validity of the AF-FA's use for assessing Tier 1 health risk requirements, only scratch the surface of answering the questions that may be examined by linking AF-FA data to health outcomes data.

---

[31] Moreover, there is little theoretical reason to believe that the nature of the relationship between the AF-FA and health and injury diagnoses would itself change. However, as suggested by a reviewer, we did execute a robustness check to determine whether controlling for occupational category would affect our main findings, and these findings did not change.

4. Perceptions of the Air Force Fitness Assessment and Culture of Fitness

In addition to analyzing the relationships between AF-FA data and various career and health outcomes, we also sought to examine perceptions of current fitness policies and the culture of fitness across the DAF. Building a more comprehensive understanding of fitness knowledge and communication, exercise habits, FA preparation, and the perceived importance of and barriers to fitness is critical to promoting a ready and deployable force. In this chapter, we summarize the views on these topics that airmen and guardians shared with us during 35 semi-structured interviews.[32]

Culture of Fitness

During interviews, airmen responded to several questions addressing the concept of a "culture of fitness" (see Appendix C for the interview protocol). These questions asked about the messages that squadron leadership had communicated and the actions that squadron leadership had taken to encourage physical fitness among members of their squadron.

Squadron Leadership Communication and Actions to Maintain Airman Fitness

Sixty percent of interviewees indicated that squadron leadership had conveyed that it was everyone's personal responsibility to stay fit. Considering variability across squadron types, we noted that members of the fighter, force support, and special operations squadrons most commonly provided this response. For example, a member (E-7, female) of a fighter squadron stated, "With this squadron, [the message] is individual responsibility, and it's not necessarily pushed but kind of like 'take care of yourself.'" The next most-common responses were that squadron leadership emphasized the importance of fitness generally (40 percent), and leadership stressed the importance of airmen taking time for physical training (PT; 26 percent).[33]

---

[32] Unless otherwise noted, all percentages reported in this chapter share the common denominator of 35 (i.e., the number of interviewees who provided a comment). These percentages indicate how often themes were mentioned by interviewees, but they should not be considered representative of the total DAF population. Individuals might have provided more than one response per topic, and these are counted within each response they provide.

[33] There was a great deal of variability in interviewees' responses to questions regarding how squadron leadership communicated these messages about physical fitness and how often they did so. Interviewees most commonly responded that these messages were communicated at commander's calls (29 percent) or by email (26 percent). Some interviewees also indicated that the information was simply communicated by word of mouth (17 percent) or via text message or a messaging application (11 percent). In addition, interviewees most commonly indicated that these messages were communicated approximately once a month (23 percent), with other interviewees indicating that the messages were communicated quarterly (14 percent) or frequently (14 percent).

Interviewees did not appear to strongly believe that squadron leadership communication about physical fitness substantially affected the physical fitness of the squadron. Approximately 26 percent of interviewees commented that messages from leadership on maintaining physical fitness had a positive impact on squadron fitness, but 17 percent indicated that these messages had no impact.

Actions Leadership Has Taken to Promote Fitness

Interviewees also discussed what actions, if any, squadron leadership had taken to ensure members of the squadron maintained physical fitness. In doing so, interviewees (66 percent) mentioned unit PT sessions. In particular, this response was most commonly provided by interviewed members of the space control, force support, electronic warfare, and special operations squadrons. For example, a member (E-8, female) of a space control squadron commented, "So pre-COVID, we actually had one organizational [activity] where everybody would meet up on Tuesdays to do PT together. It would be some sort of activity with a cardio and strength training component and then the other half of it would be something more team-building." The next most-frequently mentioned (23 percent) action taken by squadron leadership—mentioned only by interviewed members of the fighter, space control, and force support squadrons—was to provide the squadron with example workouts. For example, a member (O-3, male) of a fighter squadron commented, "Our squadron commander has recommended—like [when] we're on TDY [temporary duty travel], for example, he sent out a bodyweight workout regimen that we could do in our hotel rooms while we're gone. So, I thought that was a good thing."

Most interviewees (69 percent) also commented that their leadership provided time for them to exercise during the work week. Most of the interviewees who indicated that they received time during the duty day for exercise were members of the space control, electronic warfare, force support, and special operations squadrons. A member of a special operations squadron (O-3, male) stated, "In my last squadron, we had a mandatory PT day on Mondays. And, [in] this squadron, it's just the policy of showing up late and leaving early in order to work out three days a week."

Discussing whether these actions had any impact on fitness, almost half of the interviewees (46 percent) commented on the positive impacts on fitness. However, 31 percent of interviewees also indicated that these actions had little or no effect on squadron fitness. A member of a special operations squadron (O-3, male) stated,

> I'm sure [such actions] improved [squadron fitness] a little bit by the fact that we
> can have extra time to work out, but I don't think it makes that much of an

impact. The people that are going to work out are going to work out, and the people that aren't going to work out aren't going to work out.[34]

Rewards for Maintaining Physical Fitness and Consequences for Not Doing So

Addressing rewards for maintaining physical fitness, over half of interviewees (54 percent) indicated that they received time off, such as a one-day pass (i.e., one day off of work), for earning a composite score of 90 or above on the AF-FA. This reward was most-commonly mentioned by members of the electronic warfare, force support, air refueling, and space control squadrons. In addition, several interviewees (14 percent) indicated that airmen who received a certain score on the AF-FA (e.g., 90 or above, 100) had their name included on a squadron fitness board or otherwise announced to the squadron, and several interviewees (9 percent) indicated that squadron members who earned such scores received a hat, button, or T-shirt. However, many interviewees (34 percent) said that they received no rewards for maintaining fitness; this was most common among interviewed members of the special operations and missile squadrons. Addressing this lack of reward, a member of a special operations squadron (O-5, male) stated, "We don't reward anybody for maintaining physical fitness. It's part of your job."

In terms of consequences for poor physical fitness, about half of interviewees (51 percent) indicated that squadron members who performed poorly on the AF-FA were required to participate in a remediation program that included mandatory physical fitness. This was most commonly noted by interviewed members of the space control, fighter, and electronic warfare squadrons. Other interviewees discussed removal from the AF for repeatedly failing the AF-FA (17 percent) and the professional consequences of not receiving rewards and not being recommended for professional development opportunities if they failed the AF-FA (11 percent).

Knowledge of and Preparation for the Air Force Fitness Assessment

In addition to assessing leadership's role in influencing a culture of fitness, we also asked interviewees to discuss what they knew about the AF-FA, their impressions of the assessment, and how airmen prepare for it.

Air Force Fitness Assessment Knowledge

In discussing what airmen know about the AF-FA, most interviewees (74 percent) commented that airmen know what the four components are, and that airmen know the minimum

---

[34] In addition to discussing actions that commanders took to promote fitness, interviewees also addressed resources provided to promote fitness. In doing so, almost half (49 percent) commented on the benefits of gyms that were either in or near the squadron. In addition, many interviewees (20 percent) commented on the availability of physical fitness leaders or assistants. Describing this resource, a member (E-5, female) of a fighter squadron said,

> I don't even know what to call them, but they're some type of physical fitness assistants. And similar to that, [there are] other people who do some kind of body work or [help] you do different workouts. [Squadron leaders] brought those people in. And those are for all of the fighter squadron people, and so that has been really nice to have that availability.

scores required in each of these components (63 percent). In addition, most interviewees (86 percent) indicated that airmen are knowledgeable about the frequency with which they are required to take the AF-FA. These comments were relatively evenly distributed across members of different squadron types. Overall, this suggests that airmen likely have a good deal of knowledge about the basic requirements of the AF-FA.

We also asked interviewees if airmen knew the scientific rationale underlying the inclusion of the different AF-FA components, and most interviewees (83 percent) indicated that airmen had no knowledge of the scientific basis for including these four components. Of those interviewees who indicated that airmen had some knowledge of this rationale, 60 percent were members of a space control squadron.

Air Force Fitness Assessment Preparation

Interviewees also discussed what they and other airmen did to prepare for the AF-FA. Most interviewees (60 percent) commented that they increased fitness training in areas on which the AF-FA components focus. Addressing this point, a member (O-1, male) of a force support squadron stated, "I just look at what's required in the test and work out based off that. I think that's about it." The next most common response (34 percent) was that airmen participate in mock assessments. For example, a member (O-4, female) of a space control squadron commented that

> they typically will have a 90-, 60-, 30-day plan. So there's like a—at three months out, they'll do a practice PT test with their supervisor to get an assessment of how hard they need to work, and they'll create a plan based off of that. If one is needed, they'll do another 60-day and then a 30-day out check.

Other interviewees described a less-formal process. For example, a member (O-3, male) of a fighter squadron stated,

> I would say that they basically maintain whatever their workout regimen is, but probably closer to the fitness testing, they'll do some mock runs of the fitness test, just on their own time, just to get an idea of a baseline of where they're at and where they will score. And [they] kind of determine what they need to do to increase their score if they need to.

Time Taken to Prepare for the Fitness Assessment

Discussing how much time airmen take to prepare for the AF-FA, most interviewees (60 percent) commented that airmen begin to prepare for the assessment about two to three months before they must take it. This response was most often provided by interviewees who had 15 to 19 years of service in the AF. The next most common response across interviewees (40 percent) was that airmen begin to prepare about three to four weeks before they must take the assessment. This response was most often provided by interviewees with zero to nine years of service in the AF. Overall, these responses suggest that, often times, airmen are not maintaining the same type and level of fitness throughout the year and that the time taken to prepare for the FA might vary based on an airman's YOS, which is likely associated with age.

Harmful Actions Taken to Prepare for the Fitness Assessment

We also asked interviewees if they were aware of any potentially harmful actions taken by airmen to prepare for the AF-FA. Interviewees described multiple actions that they had seen or heard of airmen taking in preparation for the AF-FA, including

- extreme dieting or "starving" themselves (40 percent)
- wrapping their waists in plastic or Saran Wrap prior to the FA to reduce AC (20 percent)
- overexercising during the week or two before the FA (17 percent)
- taking diet pills (6 percent)
- taking laxatives (6 percent)
- going to a sauna to lose water weight (6 percent).

Impressions of the Current Air Force Fitness Assessment

In addition to discussing knowledge of and preparation for the AF-FA, interviewees provided both their personal impressions of the AF-FA and the impressions that other airmen have about the AF-FA.

Personal Impressions of the Fitness Assessment

Interviewees (37 percent) commented that the AF-FA helps to ensure minimum levels of fitness among airmen—a response that was most common among members of a fighter squadron. For example, a member (O-3, female) of the fighter squadron said, "I would say my current impression is [the AF-FA is] fair . . . it's a decent assessment if you're not going to—this might be kind of harsh to say—keel over from a heart attack or something." Another common impression among interviewees (40 percent) was that the AF-FA is not accurate or valid—a response that was most common among interviewed members of the space control and missile squadrons. For example, a member (O-3, male) of a space control squadron commented, "Brutally honest? I think it's not really a good way to assess the fitness of a person."

Some interviewees commented on the specific AF-FA components. In doing so, interviewees (23 percent) often commented that they did not like or appreciate the relevance of the AC measurement. For example, a member (E-6, male) of an electronic warfare squadron stated,

> If there would be one thing that I think is a negative, that I don't understand,
> [it's] the waist measurement part. Some people just have bigger builds, genes, or
> whatever you might call it. But if you have a 40-inch waist or a 42-inch waist and
> if you could still get out there and run a mile and a half underneath the time that
> you're supposed to, I don't see what the problem is.

In addition, several interviewees (14 percent) commented that they did not like or appreciate the relevance of the 1.5-mile run. A member (O-5, male) of a missile squadron stated

45

I don't have an overly high opinion of it. . . . My personal opinion is that it's geared towards marathon runners, so my natural assumption is that the Air Force must want marathon runners. There's a heavy, heavy weight put [on] the run and the waist component and very little given to the sit-up and push-up component[s], which to me is the physique of a marathon runner.

Barriers to Fitness

Interviewees also addressed various factors that contribute to airmen not getting enough exercise or maintaining their fitness.

General Barriers to Fitness

Discussing broad barriers to fitness, most interviewees (57 percent) commented that long work or duty hours were a barrier to fitness. This response was most frequently provided by members of the fighter, special operations, and force support squadrons. For example, a member (O-5, male) of a fighter squadron said, "I would say the first [barrier] is, for us specifically, schedule, or call it operational demand on our time. Basically, you have to be motivated to do it outside of a 10- to 12-hour duty day, to be able to actually fit it in, which is unfair to the airmen."

In addition, a member (O-3, female) of a special operations squadron stated,

> Long work hours, changing schedules, and if one thing's going to go, it's probably going to be my run first. I know, for me, one of my biggest barriers to achieving the level of fitness that I would like to maintain is time. I do best with physical fitness when I can set a regular schedule, and my schedule is anything but regular.

Other responses (mentioned by approximately 9 to 11 percent of interviewees) were that limited access to gym equipment, irregular schedules (as noted previously), lack of appreciation for physical fitness, and declining societal emphasis on sports and fitness also served as barriers.

Challenges to Fitness Because of the Installation

Asked what, if any, aspects of their installation make it a challenge to stay physically fit, almost half of interviewees (46 percent) indicated that their installation presented no challenges. However, several interviewees (34 percent) commented that aspects of the temperature or environment at their installation's location made it challenging to exercise. For example, a member (O-5, male) of a missile squadron commented,

> I think our winters here affect it—I mean, just going outside can be a deterrence. Just the climate outside is a deterrent to not leave your home, much less go to the gym, much less do something like running or playing outside [if that] is your primary physical activity, primary exercise, then it's almost not safe to do that during the wintertime.

Relatedly, a member (O-3, male) of a special operations squadron stated, "It's hot out, I guess would be the only thing I could give; is that it is very hot in Florida, so it sucks to run outside."

Readiness

During each interview, we asked airmen to discuss the association between the AF-FA and readiness, both readiness to do their jobs and readiness to deploy.

Air Force Fitness Assessment and Job Readiness

We first asked interviewees their opinion on whether the current AF-FA is an accurate or inaccurate measurement of readiness to perform the job requirements of their AFSC or career field. Most interviewees (63 percent) commented that the AF-FA was an inaccurate measurement of that. This response was most common among members of the space control and special operations squadrons. Discussing this point, a member (O-3, male) of a space control squadron commented, "It really doesn't take much level of activity to sit at a desk and monitor a computer for hours on end on shift. But regardless, it is the military, and these are the standards." Similarly, a member (O-3, female) of a special operations squadron stated, "I think it's wildly inaccurate. I have no idea what a mile-and-a-half run has to do with me trying to carve my way out of a burning airplane and get 600 feet away." Notably, however, many interviewees (31 percent) indicated that the AF-FA was an accurate measurement of job readiness. Addressing this point further, a member (O-3, male) of an air refueling squadron stated, "I think if someone can pass the minimum components of any one area, I think that's about where you want anyone to be in order to safely and efficiently do the job."

When asked how policies or practices could be changed to better support job readiness, interviewees most commonly responded (34 percent) that the DAF could redesign the AF-FA to be job or career field specific. This response was most common among members of special operations, fighter, and air refueling squadrons. For example, a member (O-3, male) of a fighter squadron commented, "Based on whatever job you have, they could vary the fitness test, I think, because certain jobs require more than others." However, a large proportion of interviewees (29 percent) indicated that no changes were needed to the AF-FA.

Air Force Fitness Assessment and Deployment Readiness

We also asked interviewees their opinion on whether the current AF-FA is an accurate or inaccurate measurement of readiness to deploy. Similar to their perceptions of job readiness, most interviewees (63 percent) said that the AF-FA was an inaccurate measurement of deployment readiness, a response that was particularly common among members of special operations, space control, and force support squadrons. However, many interviewees (34 percent) indicated that they perceived the AF-FA to be an accurate measure of deployment readiness.

Impacts of COVID-19 on Readiness

The COVID-19 pandemic affected daily lives and operations, potentially influencing readiness. During these interviews, we asked interviewees to discuss different elements of the COVID-19 impacts.

Air Force Fitness Assessment Preparation During the COVID-19 Pandemic

Addressing how the COVID-19 pandemic had affected preparation for the AF-FA, many interviewees (40 percent) commented that airmen have reduced the extent to which they work out, and many interviews (34 percent) also commented that no one was focused on the AF-FA. A member (O-3, male) of a special operations squadron noted, "I think they don't prepare any more until they know when they have to take their next test. I'd say 50/50 on that. . . . Half the people still work out; half the people are like, 'Oh, sweet, I get the year off working out.'"

Several interviewees (17 percent) commented that airmen are still preparing for the AF-FA, but they are working out only on their own. A member (O-2, male) of an electronic warfare squadron stated, "They work out more from home rather than at the facility provided by the base. That's kind of what I see."

Culture of Fitness During the COVID-19 Pandemic

Discussing how, if at all, the COVID-19 pandemic has affected the DAF's culture of fitness, most interviewees (57 percent) commented that it has become harder for airmen to go to the gym. For some, this has led to increased exercising outdoors, and for others, this has led to decreased exercising overall. For example, a member (E-8, female) of a space control squadron commented,

> With gym closures, a lot of people went to gyms off base and the gym here on base is limited. . . . I've seen more people . . . take up bike riding or take up running or whatever those other things are that they can—or hiking—to where they can just get out and go do something.

A member (O-5, male) of a missile squadron stated, "Drastically. So one [issue] is the gyms, so if your primary mode of exercise was going to a gym, you literally have nothing because all gyms are closed based off maintaining physical distancing."

Another common topic among interviewees (23 percent) was that units no longer engage in PT together. For example, a member (E-4, male) of a force support squadron stated,

> After COVID-19 hit, everyone could not do PT together. All squadrons canceled their PT sessions. So basically, they just relied on all the airmen and all the members to just do PT on their own. And the majority of the people, they can't even do that on their own anymore because most of the gyms have been closed, or they're just minimally run.

Twenty-six percent of interviewees also commented on the delay or halt of administering the AF-FA, and 34 percent of interviewees mentioned the limited concern about fitness during the pandemic. A member (O-5, male) of a fighter squadron stated,

> What I would say is the people who already had a fitness-based lifestyle still maintain their fitness, and they're probably in the same place they were before. The people who did not have a fitness-based lifestyle, my guess is [they] are not maintaining their fitness as easily or as readily because it's more difficult and because there's no motivation without knowing there's a PT test coming up for them to maintain the same level of fitness.

Barriers to Fitness During the COVID-19 Pandemic

When asked to describe the primary barriers to fitness associated with the COVID-19 pandemic, interviewees repeated or complemented their previous comments made when discussing the DAF's culture of fitness. Most interviewees (71 percent) discussed the challenges of working out in a gym, such that most gyms were closed or had limited capacity. Several interviewees (14 percent) also mentioned that the pandemic had prevented unit and group exercise sessions, which subsequently decreased the amount of time that members in the unit devoted to physical fitness.

Potential Changes

Throughout the interviews, we solicited thoughts on what changes, if any, the DAF might make to better promote fitness and healthy behaviors, reduce barriers, and improve readiness.

Options to Better Promote a Culture of Fitness

Leadership Promotion of a Culture of Fitness

Assessing leadership's promotion of a culture of fitness, we asked interviewees what squadron leadership could do to make it easier for airmen in their squadron to stay physically fit and to better promote physical fitness. The most commonly provided suggestions for making it easier to stay physically fit were for leadership to provide time during the duty day that squadron members could use to work out (43 percent) and hold group physical training sessions (20 percent) during which members of the unit exercised together. Other interviewees recommended holding fun activities or competitions (11 percent), communicating nutrition information (9 percent), or communicating workout routines (9 percent).

We also asked interviewees whether they were aware of any promising physical fitness programs. Although most interviewees (60 percent) were not aware of any, some interviewees suggested holding fitness sessions via video applications (11 percent) and using mock test scores as official AF-FA scores (9 percent). For example, a member (O-3, male) of a fighter squadron commented,

> They implemented a program, like a practice PT test essentially, where airmen, before they're due for their PT tests, they can take practice tests as many times as they want to. If they pass, they're able to use that as their score. I thought that was a good thing and a way of, like, taking the pressure off a little bit of airmen.

Other suggestions that were mentioned by one or two interviewees included having child care at the base gym and mandatory fitness for anyone who fails the AF-FA.

Using the Air Force Fitness Assessment to Promote a Culture of Fitness

We also asked interviewees how the AF-FA, including information about the assessment, might be changed to better promote fitness.

Changing Components of the Fitness Assessment

Discussing what changes, if any, should be made to the AF-FA components, interviewees (37 percent) proposed that measurement of AC should be removed. However, the next most common response (23 percent) was that no changes should be made. Other suggestions were to make the components assessed in the AF-FA specific to the requirements of one's job or duty (11 percent) and to have alternatives to the 1.5-mile run (11 percent). Addressing duty-specific requirements, a member (O-5, male) of a fighter squadron commented,

> I think it should be completely replaced with a functional test that is geared towards movements and actions that you would expect to see in a—I hate to use the word "combat"—but a combat scenario. That, and/or switch it to an AFSC-specific test, in which case you would give the test towards those things need[ed] to do your job. And then for us it would be more of a strength-based test.

Discussing alternatives to the 1.5-mile run, a member (O-3, female) of an air refueling squadron stated,

> Not everybody's a runner, and I think that there should be other ways to measure aerobic fitness. I would much rather swim than run. Running is painful. You can force everybody to be a runner at the cost of them hurting themselves. And you see that a lot with shin splints and people who have hip or ankle problems and stuff like that. And so, if you were really concerned with my aerobic capabilities, then you should give me another option for that. Or if you were really concerned with my ability to run 600 meters to get out of the way of a "firefight," then that's what should be tested. Not a mile-and-a-half run. There is nothing I am ever going to do in my career that requires me to run a mile and a half.

Providing Additional Information on the Fitness Assessment

When asked what, if any, additional information that they might like to receive on the AF-FA, 54 percent of interviewees stated that they would like more information on how and why the different components and standards were chosen, a response that was relatively evenly distributed across members of different squadron types. Addressing this point, a member (O-3, male) of a fighter squadron stated,

I think it would be good to give airmen a better understanding of what each section is really testing. That way, when they go out and take a PT test, they're not just doing it just to do it. [They know it] is validated with an explanation of, "Hey, this is scientifically why we're testing each of these things the way that we do."

Reducing Harmful Actions Taken to Prepare for the Fitness Assessment

Discussing what actions might be taken to reduce harmful actions taken to prepare for the AF-FA, interviewees (23 percent) proposed that the AF better educate airmen about how to prepare for the AF-FA and the potential risks involved with taking harmful actions to prepare. This response was relatively evenly distributed across members of different squadron types. Interviewees (20 percent) also suggested that the AF should reduce the negative consequences associated with failing the AF-FA, by adjusting the implications of failing the test. For example, a member (O-4, male) of a special operations squadron commented,

I think one of the biggest things I've heard, which I thought was actually a fairly smart idea, was doing a no-repercussions fitness test. . . . So, if you take a fitness test at the beginning of the month that you're due and you fail it, you go, 'Okay, you failed it. These are the areas you work at. You now have six weeks to bring those areas up to par and the next one will have repercussions if you don't pass it.' I think that would probably be reasonable—and if you pass it that first time, it counts. You don't have to come back and test again.

Additional suggestions, provided by only one or two interviewees, included better incorporating physical fitness into one's duty day, increasing the hours during which the gym is open, and giving the AF-FA on a random basis. Other interviewees proposed that harmful actions taken in preparation for the AF-FA are unavoidable (14 percent) and that the AF should simply maintain its current practices (14 percent).

Options to Address Fitness Barriers

Interviewees also proposed what the AF could do to address the barriers to fitness that they had observed. The most commonly mentioned action (26 percent) was to provide time for airmen to exercise during the duty day. For example, a member (O-5, male) of an air refueling squadron said,

I think if they emphasized that same kind of culture that we're trying to do in the squadron, just that folks will have time during the day, I think that would help to make like an official Air Force policy. There's some verbiage about that in the AFI, but it's more of a "should" versus a "will." So they could potentially do that, just make it more clear.

Other suggestions—mentioned by 6 to 9 percent of interviewees—included providing more fitness facilities and equipment, increasing communication about the importance of physical fitness, encouraging individual responsibility for fitness, better considering the medical issues of airmen, and reducing the pressure placed on airmen to pass the AF-FA.

Interviewees also proposed changes that could be made to improve readiness.

Year-Round Readiness

Specifically, we asked interviewees to discuss how the AF can better use the AF-FA to encourage airmen to stay physically fit throughout the year, thereby promoting year-round readiness. One response (17 percent) was to increase incentives for achieving high scores on the AF-FA, such as by providing time off or monetary awards. Another suggestion was to increase the frequency at which the test is administered (14 percent). A member (O-2, female) of a force support squadron commented, "This is going to sound awful, because I'm one of those people that benefits from it, but if they want people to be healthy throughout the year, then we probably shouldn't be doing tests once a year. Although, I do love my once-a-year testing."

Other suggestions provided by one to three interviewees included using performance on the AF-FA to develop a plan for each airman, making the assessment pass/fail (rather than providing scores), randomizing the timing of the AF-FA for each airman, and holding more mock fitness tests throughout the year.

Deployment Readiness

Asked how policies or practices could be changed to better support deployment readiness, interviewees recommended changing the FA requirements for those who deploy (17 percent) and to change the components for those who deploy (17 percent). Addressing changing the FA requirements for those who deploy, a member (E-5, female) of a refueling squadron stated,

> I think that would have to depend on what the required duties are in that specific deployed location. . . . In my job, I would have to volunteer for a deployment in order to go on one. But for someone who deploys all the time, their requirements would be a lot different than mine because they are in the environment more than I would be.

Discussing changing the FA components for those who deploy, a member (O-5, male) of a missile squadron stated,

> That's where the Army has a PT test that better tailors to the job. If we had multiple events and not everybody has to do every event based off where their readiness is, where their AEF [Air and Expeditionary Force] cycle or what potential jobs they could deploy to, so maybe this gets back here we have a less efficient but more effective PT test. Because right now we have super-efficient [be]cause it's everybody does everything and it's super-simple.

What the Air Force Should Do When It Resumes Fitness Assessments After the Pandemic

Because of the potential impacts of the COVID-19 pandemic on physical fitness and readiness, we asked what, if anything, the AF should do when it resumes administering the AF-FA (i.e., when COVID-19 restrictions have been lifted). Several interviewees (29 percent) proposed that the AF should provide airmen with a few months grace period in which they have more time to prepare for the assessment or failures on assessments taken soon after they begin to be administered again do not have negative impacts on an airman's career. Commenting on the grace-period proposal, a member (E-5, female) of an air refueling squadron stated,

> I feel like there should be some type of grace period because I feel like a lot of members that are going to test in the next coming month, they're still not prepared—such as myself. And I think that I would fail a fitness assessment, but I'm pretty sure that a lot of members aren't ready, and they probably would fail the assessment. So, I feel there should be some type of grace period for a few months where we should still be able to get ourselves together after things are opening back up and just give us that time to reacclimate to getting into shape.

Several interviewees (17 percent) also commented on the importance of administering the assessment safely. A member (O-5, male) of a special operations squadron commented,

> I would not administer the test [or] anything that requires close contact of airmen until we're fully past [the need for] some of the protective measures we're doing for COVID. So, if they need to adjust some things to administer tests to make sure people aren't in each other faces, then they need to do that.

Relatedly, a member (O-3, female) of an air refueling squadron suggested,

> I think obviously limiting the number of people that are taking the fitness assessment at one time. I've taken fitness assessments before where there've been like 20 other people in the room, and you're paired up and it seems like there are two FSS [force support squadron] individuals who are administering the PT test. I think allowing the squadrons to administer their own PT test would help immensely because then they could do it on their own time, multiple days during the week, versus what is normally the standard where the gym and the FSS individuals run a PT test like Tuesdays [and] Thursdays at like three different times and you have to sign up for one of the times online. I think if squadrons could administer their own PT tests that would help out a lot.

Summary

Semi-structured interviews with 35 airmen across various squadron types provided insights into their knowledge and perceptions of the AF-FA (summarized in Table 4.1). Overall, these interviews provided information on a variety of common views among interviewees, but their views should not be interpreted as representative of the entire DAF population. These results suggest that active duty members have little knowledge of why they must complete the AF-FA or why any of the AF-FA components have been included in the assessment. In addition, there is a great deal of variability in interviewees' perceptions of the AF-FA and its components: Some interviewees perceive the standards as being too strict while others perceive them as being too lenient. Furthermore, interviewees indicated that finding time to exercise is a barrier to fitness, and they proposed that providing time during the duty day to work out and regular unit PT can assist with addressing this barrier.

Table 4.1. Overview of Interviewee Responses

Topic		Summary of Findings

Culture of fitness	Squadron leadership	• Communication: Squadron leadership tends to communicate that it is everyone's responsibility to stay fit.
		  ○ Unit members do not believe that current leadership communication about fitness affects the squadron's fitness levels.
		• Actions: Squadron leadership often uses unit PT to promote fitness and provides time for unit members to exercise during the work week.
		  ○ Unit members have varied opinions on the potential impact of leadership's actions to promote fitness.
		• Rewards/consequences: Leadership provides time off for high performers and remediation for low performers on the AF-FA.

	Knowledge of and preparation for the AF-FA	• Most airmen know what the AF-FA components are, the minimum required scores for each component, and how often they must take the AF-FA.
		  ○ Most airmen do not know the scientific rationale for including each component.
		• To prepare for the AF-FA, airmen increase their fitness training, focusing on AF-FA components, and often take about two to three months to prepare.
		  ○ Airmen might take harmful actions to prepare for the AF-FA, including extreme dieting and wrapping their waists with plastic wrap.

	Impressions	• Opinions of the AF-FA vary: Some perceive it as not valid, and some suggest that it ensures minimum fitness levels.
Barriers to fitness		• Long work or duty hours are perceived as a barrier to fitness. • Installation environment (e.g., extreme cold, heat) can also be a barrier to fitness.
Readiness		• The AF-FA is not perceived to be an accurate measure of job readiness or deployment readiness.
Potential changes		• Interviewees suggested providing time during the duty day to work out and holding group PT to encourage fitness. • To reduce harmful actions taken to prepare for the AF-FA, some suggested better educating airmen about how to prepare for the AF-FA and the risks of such actions.

54

5. Discussion and Recommendations

This project evaluated the validity and perceived relevance of the AF-FA. In doing so, we examined the relationships between AF-FA component scores—namely, for AC, the 1.5-mile run, and the timed sit-up and push-up tests—and both career and health outcomes. We found that airmen fitness, as assessed by WHtR, which is more suitable for fitter populations, has generally improved over the past 15 years. We also found that AF-FA component scores are positively associated with early- and mid-career outcomes, and the strength of association is greatest for cardiorespiratory fitness (i.e., aerobic fitness), as assessed by the 1.5-mile run. Moreover, we found that scores on most of the components are associated with health outcomes, including but not limited to various cardiovascular disease diagnoses, but sit-ups are less consistently related to these health outcomes. Finally, we found that fitness risk levels (as defined by AFI 36-2905, 2020) effectively distinguish airman health risks. Despite the relatively young and healthy airman population, Tier 1 fitness standards, based on a general consideration of health risk levels, are shown to be useful at predicting multiple relevant outcomes.

Examining airman knowledge and perceptions of the AF-FA, we found that interviewed airmen and guardians, including squadron commanders, do not understand the overall purpose of the AF-FA nor do they understand why each AF-FA component has been included in the assessment. Furthermore, views among interviewees varied widely with regard to the AF-FA and its components. Many of our interviewees did not appreciate the relevance of the AC measurement to airman fitness. Some interviewees indicated that the standards were too strict, and others indicated that they were too lenient. Some interviewees had negative opinions of the 1.5-mile run, but few commented on the inclusion of either sit-ups or push-ups in the AF-FA.

Drawing from our results, we provide several recommendations for improving the validity of AF-FA components and acceptance of the AF-FA among airmen.

Recommendations

Ensure Airmen Understand Why They Are Completing Both the Overall Fitness Assessment and Each of Its Components

As noted above, responses from interviewees suggest that many airmen and guardians (including commanders who are potentially responsible for encouraging a culture of fitness) have little or no knowledge about the overall purpose of the AF-FA, nor do they understand the reasons underlying the inclusion of each of its components. This finding was consistent across ranks; commanders were also unclear about the relevance of the AF-FA components. In other words, airmen and guardians are regularly being tested for reasons that they do not understand,

and similarly, commanders are being asked to enforce fitness standards without understanding why. To address this knowledge gap, airmen and guardians should periodically receive information regarding the DAF's intent for the AF-FA and each of its components. For example, the DAF might provide airmen with this information each time they must schedule or complete an AF-FA. Frequent and widespread provision of this information will help to increase the transparency of a currently opaque process and ensure a common understanding of both the purpose and utility of the AF-FA among DAF members.[35]

Importantly, the DAF will need to clearly establish and publicize its own goals for the AF-FA, and this information will need to be clearly communicated to and by commanders. If commanders are not aware of or have contrary opinions about the intent of this assessment, then unit members whom they lead are unlikely to understand or appreciate the relevance of the requirement to regularly complete the AF-FA.

Consider Whether and How to Inform Airmen and Guardians About Their Predicted Health-Related Risks Based on Their AF-FA Scores

As part of increasing knowledge about the purpose of the AF-FA and its components, the DAF might consider informing each airman and guardian of their predicted health-related risks, based on their AF-FA scores. However, the utility in providing this information remains unclear. Previous research suggests that airmen with higher health risks demonstrate greater short-term anxiety, distress, and poorer perceptions of health than they did before being informed of their health risks, although there is no evidence for longer-term effects (Shaw, Abrams, and Marteau, 1999). One way to manage such concerns might be to provide evidence-based recommendations and a fitness plan with their personal health-risk information to mitigate such effects (Marteau and Lerman, 2001). Research suggests that participation in employer-sponsored health and well-being programs is associated with decreases in health risks (Seaverson et al., 2019). More generally, one option might be to provide risk-related information only to airmen and guardians who want this information after completing the AF-FA, allowing them to make an informed choice about whether they receive information on their predicted health risks (Marteau, 2002).

Continue Measuring, Recording, and Reporting on Abdominal Circumference

We found that the AC component score was associated with both career and health outcomes for airmen. Although many interviewees had negative opinions of this particular AF-FA component, its observed associations with relevant outcomes suggest that the DAF should continue to track AC, regardless of whether it continues to be included as a component in the AF-FA. An integrated system for monitoring airman AC could help the DAF plan specific interventions to increase physical activity and fitness. Furthermore, AC could be used as a

---

[35] At the time of this research, the U.S. Space Force was considering various options for its FA, including use of a different assessment than the AF-FA.

leading indicator of health service and provider requirements across the DAF because of AC's established relationships with various diagnoses, even in the DAF's relatively young and healthy active duty population.

Promote a Culture of Fitness Through Leadership Support for Physical Fitness During the Workday/Duty Hours

Our research also suggests that the DAF needs to take additional steps to better promote a culture of fitness among its members. Discussing challenges of maintaining physical fitness, many interviewees commented on the limited available time during the duty day to work out, and when providing their own recommendations for improving unit fitness, they proposed that receiving time during the workday/duty hours, which might include unit PT, would help airmen and guardians to stay fit. Indeed, previous research among civilians suggests that, overall, worksite interventions can help to increase employee levels of physical activity (Taylor, Conner, and Lawton, 2012), and in particular, coworker support has significant positive effects on physical activity (Pedersen, Halvari, and Olafsen, 2019).

If unit leadership allows airmen to take time during the workday (e.g., provide duty hours to work out), they could consider implementing measures to track what airmen and guardians are doing to stay fit and how often they are engaging in these activities. This information would provide leadership with the ability to help unit members implement effective physical fitness plans, and it would help to ensure that airmen and guardians are held accountable for using the provided time to work out. Furthermore, if data were collected systematically across units, this information could assist the DAF with tracking health outcomes from these programs and the associated costs.

In addition, if unit leadership implements or continues unit PT, consideration might need to be given to the variability in physical fitness levels and abilities among unit members. For example, airmen who already work out regularly and have not had recent injuries might require or prefer a more rigorous PT session than airmen who do not work out as vigorously. By contrast, airmen who have traditionally engaged in less physical activity or who have recently been injured might require exercises more tailored to their current abilities and more time to reach a higher level of physical fitness. Among other things, this consideration of abilities could help to reduce the number and severity of injuries and potentially reduce overweight stigma for airmen who may be less fit (Vartanian and Shaprow, 2008).

Consider Rewarding Units That Regularly Engage in Physical Activity Rather Than Focusing on Providing Incentives That Are Based on Fitness Assessment Scores

To promote more consistent engagement in physical activity, the DAF should consider providing incentives based on measures other than the AF-FA scores. Interviewees indicated that they did not begin preparing for the AF-FA until a few weeks or months before they would be required to take it, and many commented on the lack of fitness training during the COVID-19 pandemic, in part because of the lack of an AF-FA for which they had to prepare. This suggests that the AF-FA does not encourage airmen to consistently work out throughout the year. One way to better promote fitness might be to reward units that can clearly demonstrate that their members regularly engage in physical activity. This would continue to provide airmen and guardians with incentives to work out, moving beyond their AF-FA scores, and encourage group behavior around physical fitness training, so that unit members may be more likely to participate in physical fitness activities of their unit (Pearson et al., 2020).

Conclusions

To answer the questions that motivated this study, we provide the following conclusions:

- How relevant are civilian results that link fitness to health and career outcomes to the DAF, which has a relatively young and fit population?

  - These links are relevant for a variety of health and career outcomes among airmen.

- What are the relationships between specific AF-FA components and health outcomes?

  - These relationships vary across health outcomes and time frames considered, but they are strongest for the AC and 1.5-mile run components and weakest for the sit-ups component. Poorer component performance is more strongly associated with an increased risk of receiving health diagnoses than injury diagnoses.

- What are the relationships between specific AF-FA components and career outcomes?

  - These relationships vary across career outcomes considered, but they are strongest for the AC and 1.5-mile run components. Poorer component performance is associated with lower retention and poorer career outcomes.

- Does the AF-FA scoring system differentiate between levels of health risk?

  - Yes, airmen who are considered to be at high risk, based on their AF-FA component scores, have a higher probability of being diagnosed with various adverse health outcomes.

Our evidence-based recommendations offer immediate actions that the DAF can take to address some long-standing questions about AF-FA standards. Our health outcomes analyses, for example, controlled for only basic health indicators that were available throughout the analytical time period. However, a more comprehensive assessment could include health-relevant behaviors, such as ongoing physical activity, alcohol and tobacco use, and nutrition habits, to provide tailored risk-reduction activities to meet individual airman needs. In addition, our analyses focused on only a subset of relevant health outcomes, although other relevant diagnoses may be of interest.

Because our study was intended to evaluate Tier 1 fitness standards, we did not consider predeployment (Tier 1-D) or mission-specific fitness standards in our analyses.[36] However, our qualitative results suggest that in addition to communicating clearly about the general health risk-reduction utility of Tier 1 fitness standards to airmen, developing further fitness standards to better reflect deployment or job-based demands might have appeal. Our findings concerning the Tier 1 fitness standards suggest that higher fidelity assessments might be even better at predicting important health and career outcomes among airmen.

---

[36] See Robson et al., 2020, to learn more about how RAND has assisted the AF's development and validation of gender-neutral tests and standards for six battlefield airmen specialties.

Appendix A. Ancillary Analysis of Fitness Data

In this appendix, we describe the steps that we took to prepare the AF-FA data for analysis. We then present results from additional analysis.

Air Force Fitness Management System Data Preparation

Nonexempt airmen are required to complete the AF-FA at least once per year. However, many airmen complete the AF-FA multiple times per year. For example, airmen who receive a satisfactory or unsatisfactory composite score must repeat the AF-FA biannually and within 90 calendar days, respectively. In our data, approximately 35 percent of airmen repeated the AF-FA within a single year. To collapse data into person-year records, we took the average of an individual's scores from all assessments completed in the same year.[37]

The data contained a small number of implausible values. To correct for outliers, we excluded the most extreme 1 percent of values for all AF-FA components (i.e., upper and lower 0.5 percent of values). In addition, a small percentage of component scores were not recorded for nonexempt airmen. Table A.1 shows the overall percentages of missing values (outliers plus nonrecorded values) by AF-FA component. Given that the data were missing completely at random, we imputed missing values using the Amelia package in R (R Core Team, 2019). Amelia assumes that data are drawn from a multivariate normal distribution, and it uses an expectation-maximization algorithm with bootstrapping to impute missing values (Honaker, King, and Blackwell, 2011).

Table A.1. Percentages of Missing Scores and Exemptions by AF-FA Component

AF-FA Component	Missing Score (%)	Exemption (%)	Combined (%)
AC	1.2	2.7	3.9
1.5-mile run	1.0	13.0	14.0
Push-ups	1.3	7.9	9.2
Sit-ups	1.3	7.4	8.7

Airmen may be excluded from select components of the AF-FA in a specific year. To determine annual exemptions, we treated an airman as exempt from a component if they were exempt from the component throughout the full year and as nonexempt otherwise. In the case of

---

[37] In some instances, airmen had duplicate records from the same test date. We combined these into a single record by taking the maximum of an individual's scores from all assessments completed on the same date.

60

the aerobic component, we treated an airman as exempt if they were exempt from the 1.5-mile run, even if they participated in an alternate aerobic assessment (e.g., the 2.0-kilometer walk). Table A.1 shows the overall percentages of exemptions by AF-FA component. Exemptions were rare in the first YOS; thus, for analyses that used initial fitness levels, we excluded records with exemptions. Exemptions were more common in later YOS; thus, for analyses of annual outcomes (i.e., retention and eligibility for deployment), we retained records with exemptions and included exemption status as a predictor variable.

Airmen may also be excluded from all AF-FA components in a specific year. To determine these composite exemptions, we treated an airman as exempt if they were exempt from all AF-FA components throughout the full year. There are multiple causes for composite exemptions and not all are negative (e.g., pregnancy or deployment). For that reason, and because causes for composite exemptions were not always provided, we excluded records with composite exemptions. That amounted to 2.7 percent of records.[38]

To analyze the effects of component scores on annual and career outcomes, we fitted two logistic regression models to each outcome. The first model predicted the outcome based on an airman's exemption status from each of the four fitness components. We then fitted a second model for airmen who were nonexempt from all four fitness components. The second model predicted outcomes for nonexempt airmen based on the four component scores. Because exemptions were so infrequent in the first YOS, we only fitted the second set of models in the case of career outcomes. The models controlled for several variables: YOS, AFSC, gender, rank type (officer or enlisted), and, for some analyses, length of initial service commitment.

Additional Fitness Analysis

Table A.2 contains regression coefficients estimated for all career and annual outcomes. Two sets of coefficients are reported for annual outcomes: The first set corresponds to component scores, and the second set corresponds to exemption status. A single set of coefficients is reported for career outcomes, corresponding to component scores in the first YOS. In all analyses, we standardized scores, meaning that the reported coefficients show the expected increase in the log-odds of the outcome for each one-unit change in the score.[39] Positive values denote an increased likelihood of the outcome, and negative values denote a decreased likelihood.

Completing each component was associated with a large increase in the log-odds of positive annual and career outcomes. Of the component scores, performance in the 1.5-mile run was

---

[38] For comparison, exemptions from the AC measurement are rare. The total percentage of composite exemptions nearly equaled the percentage of AC exemptions (Table A.1), meaning that most airmen who were exempt from the AC measurement in a specific year were exempt from the entire AF-FA.

[39] We standardized scores separately within the four subgroups formed by crossing gender (male and female) and rank (officer and enlisted).

associated with the largest increases in the log-odds of positive outcomes. Scores for the push-ups component was also consistently associated with smaller increases in the log-odds of all outcomes. Finally, scores for the sit-ups and AC components were inconsistently associated with small changes in the log-odds of all outcomes.

Table A.2. Regression Coefficients for Career and Annual Outcome Models

Variable/ Measure	AF-FA Component	Career Outcome				Annual Outcome	
		First-Term Completion	Early E-5 Promotion	SOS Top-Third	Ever Executive	Retention	Deployability
Score	Sit-ups	−0.05*	0.04**	0.02	0.02	0.09*	−0.07*
Score	Push-ups	0.05*	0.13*	0.19*	0.07*	0.06*	0.05*
Score	AC	0.05*	−0.05*	−0.04	−0.02	0.05*	0.08*
Score	1.5-mile run	0.10*	0.24*	0.37*	0.08*	0.17*	0.18*
Completion	Sit-ups					0.38*	0.44*
Completion	Push-ups					0.43*	0.66*
Completion	AC					0.26*	0.62*
Completion	1.5-mile run					0.24*	0.91*

NOTE: *$p < 0.05$; **$p < 0.01$

Table A.3 shows the means and standard deviations that we used to standardize AF-FA component scores.

Table A.3. Means and Standard Deviations Used to Standardize AF-FA Component Scores

Variable/ Measure	AF-FA Component	Officers		Enlisted Personnel	
		Female	Male	Female	Male
Annual	Sit-ups	48.0 (7.8)	52.6 (6.7)	45.2 (8.5)	52 (8)
Annual	Push-ups	36.0 (9.9)	52.8 (9.4)	32.4 (9.7)	52.7 (10.1)
Annual	AC	29.3 (2.6)	33.7 (2.7)	29.9 (2.8)	33.5 (3)
Annual	1.5-mile run	791.1 (98.3)	686.2 (79.2)	853.9 (100.4)	722 (85.9)
Career (1st YOS)	Sit-ups	52.6 (6.2)	56.9 (5.3)	47.9 (7.1)	54.7 (7.4)
Career (1st YOS)	Push-ups	38.9 (8.4)	59.6 (8.3)	33.9 (8.6)	54.2 (10.3)
Career (1st YOS)	AC	28.7 (2.3)	32.2 (2.4)	28.9 (2.3)	31.5 (2.2)
Career (1st YOS)	1.5-mile run	762.6 (83.4)	653.2 (69)	796.2 (77.9)	657 (63.8)

NOTE: Standard deviations are shown in parentheses.

Figures A.1 through A.4 show the predicted probabilities generated by the statistical models for the four career outcomes based on gender, rank type, and performance on each of the AF-FA components during the first YOS.

Figure A.1. Relationship Between First-Term Completion and Fitness Performance of Enlisted Personnel

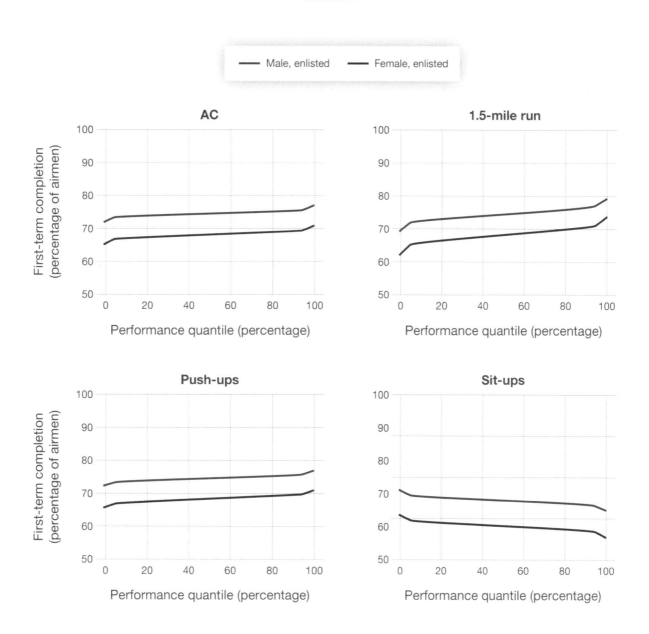

Figure A.2. Relationship Between First-Term Promotion and Fitness Performance of Enlisted Personnel

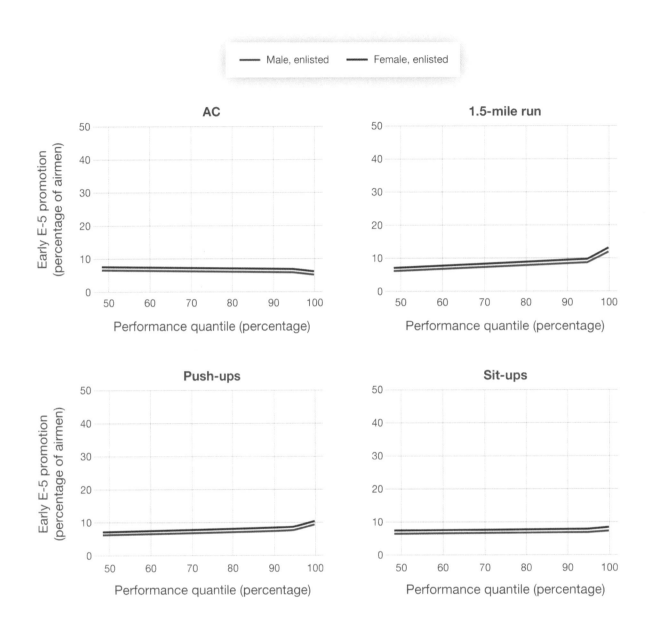

Figure A.3. Relationship Between Graduating in the Top-Third of Squadron Officer School and Fitness Performance of Officers

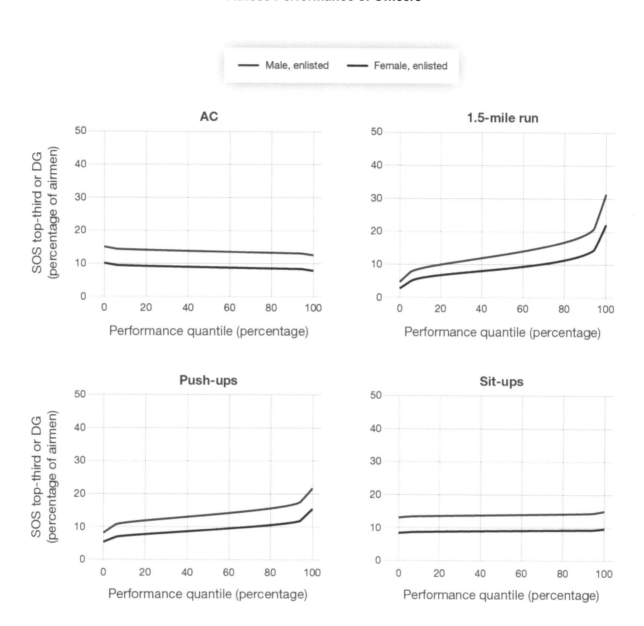

NOTE: DG = distinguished graduate.

Figure A.4. Relationship Between Ever Executive and Fitness Performance of Officers

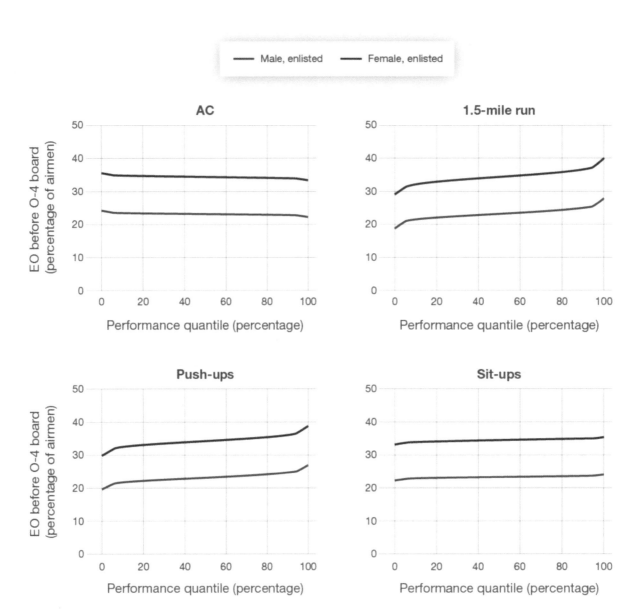

NOTE: EO = executive officer.

Appendix B. Additional Details on Health Data, Logistic Regression, and Survival Analysis Results

This appendix provides additional details on the analyses underlying Chapter 3. These include the classification method that we used to assign ICD codes to health and injury diagnosis categories, which were used to develop the dependent variables in the analyses of health outcomes. To develop the categories, we began with the CCS classification method for ICD-9 and ICD-10 codes. We made further adjustments to the classification based on discussion with clinical experts and reviews of the literature, where applicable. A table showing the resulting categories used to derive the indicators for each health outcome used in the analysis is available upon request.

We next describe our analytic approach in more detail.

Analytic Approach

Multivariate Logistic Regression

First, we used multivariate logistic regression analyses to examine how well airmen's fitness in their first YOS predicted the occurrence of a *new* health diagnosis in their second YOS. By predicting future diagnoses, this analysis helps avoid concerns of reverse causality (i.e., that the health condition itself led to a decline in fitness).[40] The full odds ratios from the logistic regression model are shown here in Appendix B, and select odds ratios are shown in the tables in Chapter 3.[41] These analyses establish an understanding of the relevance of the AF-FA, even for airmen early in their careers when the risk of negative health events is at its lowest. Although these analyses explore evidence that fitness scores in an airmen's first year can be used to predict the likelihood of diagnosis in the following year, fitness levels change over time and many airmen may reenlist and serve for more than one term. To address these points, we conducted survival analysis that considers changes in fitness levels over time. Survival analysis is a common approach in health-related fields in which the probability of an event is modeled, prototypically, as survival or death. However, in the current context, survival means an airman does not receive one of the specific diagnoses that we include in our analysis.

---

[40] The focus on new (i.e., incident) diagnoses reduces but does not eliminate the concern that airmen's physical health conditions may have affected their performance on the prior AF-FA.

[41] Odds ratios greater than 1 indicate an increased likelihood of the binary outcome (receipt of a diagnosis) as the predictor variable increases, while odds ratios less than 1 indicate that the likelihood of the outcome decreases.

Kaplan-Meier Estimates

For the survival analyses, we adapted low-, moderate-, and high-risk fitness categories based on the AF-FA scoring system (AFI 36-2905, 2020) for each of the four AF-FA components. Fitness scores for AC and cardiorespiratory endurance (i.e., the 1.5-mile run) are determined by AF standards, which we used to generate cutoffs for approximately equivalent fitness categories for push-ups and sit-ups. For AC, standards vary by gender, and for the 1.5-mile run, standards vary by gender and age. The Kaplan-Meier estimates were used to determine the expected rates of health and injury diagnoses for airmen in different fitness categories.[42]

Cox Proportional-Hazards Model

In our final set of analyses, we explored the hazard ratios for adverse health outcomes based on different fitness levels. Because we updated airmen's fitness categories over time, we cannot produce predicted Kaplan-Meier survival curves or incidence estimates because airmen are no longer part of one fixed fitness category over their whole service. Instead, we use a Cox proportional-hazards model to estimate hazard ratios of receiving a health diagnosis based on an airman's current fitness. The hazard ratios show the amount of increased likelihood of diagnosis for airmen who are in the moderate- or high-risk category compared with airmen in the low-risk category on that fitness component.

Detailed Results

Tables B.1 through B.5 present odds ratios from the logistic regressions that we used to derive the predicted probabilities discussed in Chapter 3. These tables present the models with all coefficients, including controls. Unless otherwise noted, the results presented in this appendix are based on our analysis of DHA data linked to AFPC and AF-FA data from FY 2004 to FY 2015.

The main form of the model, which we discuss in Chapter 3, is presented in Table B.3, in columns marked YOS = 2, in which analyses are restricted to airmen in their first two YOS. This main model first examines the relationship between fitness scores and health outcomes in the first and second year observed, respectively.

Table B.1 is a similar table for the analysis of exemptions, with the full list of coefficients for the model discussed in this report.

---

[42] In the same way as the previous section, we limited our data to the years that used ICD-9 codes, but instead of looking at only second-year fitness scores, these models consider the full fitness record of each airman. In survival models, our outcome is the number of days from the start of an airman's record, in this case their first fitness assessment date, until either a diagnosis or the end of their record (i.e., censored either because they left the service or reached the end of our date range without a diagnosis).

Table B.1. Odds Ratios of the Effect of AF-FA Component Exemptions on New Diagnoses in the Following Year

AF-FA Component Exemption	Hypertension	Other Cardiovascular Disease	Diabetes	Overuse Injuries	Other Musculoskeletal Conditions
AC exemption	0.915	0.808*	0.795	1.935*	1.096
	(0.083)	(0.044)	(0.125)	(0.110)	(0.056)
1.5-mile run exemption	1.255*	1.097**	1.764*	0.727*	0.816*
	(0.088)	(0.048)	(0.238)	(0.028)	(0.033)
Sit-ups exemption	1.167	1.080	0.869	0.684*	0.924
	(0.106)	(0.059)	(0.182)	(0.032)	(0.046)
Push-ups exemption	0.918	1.173**	1.551**	0.844*	1.079
	(0.097)	(0.074)	(0.329)	(0.046)	(0.063)
Demographic Variable					
Asian or Pacific Islander	1.265*	0.839*	1.588*	0.931*	1.006
	(0.074)	(0.024)	(0.189)	(0.019)	(0.021)
Black	1.422*	1.121*	1.464*	1.038*	1.052*
	(0.042)	(0.017)	(0.098)	(0.012)	(0.012)
Hispanic	0.832*	0.926*	1.425*	1.055*	1.062*
	(0.039)	(0.017)	(0.124)	(0.013)	(0.014)
Other race	1.190**	0.952	1.608*	1.056**	1.015
	(0.087)	(0.035)	(0.236)	(0.028)	(0.028)
Enlisted	1.421*	1.243*	1.526*	1.383*	1.526*
	(0.047)	(0.020)	(0.112)	(0.017)	(0.020)
Ever deployed	0.801*	0.711*	0.581*	0.700*	0.682*
	(0.025)	(0.011)	(0.048)	(0.008)	(0.008)
Height	0.922*	0.979*	0.907*	0.991*	0.992*
	(0.004)	(0.002)	(0.010)	(0.002)	(0.002)
Weight	1.020*	1.007*	1.017*	1.005*	1.006*
	(0.001)	(0.000)	(0.001)	(0.000)	(0.000)
Age	1.082*	1.028*	1.093*	1.020*	1.009*
	(0.004)	(0.002)	(0.009)	(0.001)	(0.002)
YOS	1.000	0.988*	0.991	0.989*	0.984*
	(0.004)	(0.002)	(0.008)	(0.002)	(0.002)
Female	0.952	1.422*	1.776*	1.411*	1.175*
	(0.040)	(0.025)	(0.143)	(0.018)	(0.016)
Observations (*n*)	497,628	497,628	497,628	497,628	497,628

NOTE: We estimated the logistic regression model by using AF-FA component exemptions and demographic characteristics in the first year observed and new diagnoses in the second year observed. This model includes airmen of all YOS and focuses on ICD-9 diagnoses (FY 2004–FY 2015); airmen with exemptions for pregnancy and deployment are excluded. Standard errors are shown in parentheses. * $p < 0.05$; **$p < 0.01$.

Sensitivity Analyses

There could be a different relationship between fitness and health outcomes for airmen at different points in their career. To test this, we estimated the multivariate models separately, looking at outcomes specifically for airmen in their first YOS and compared this with airmen at later points in their career.

Tables B.2 through B.5 show that, in general, the magnitude and the statistical significance of the relationship between various AF-FA components and health outcomes remains similar across comparisons. There are a few exceptions. First, Table B.2 shows that the results are persistent over time: The odds ratios are of similar magnitude, direction, and significance when predicting health outcomes two years later instead of in the following year. Table B.3 compares the results for airmen in their second YOS with airmen who are observed in later points in their careers. In general, the results show a similar pattern for airmen at different points in their careers, although there are some notable differences. First, the odds ratio on AC is actually larger for airmen in later points in their careers than for airmen in their second YOS. Run time is predictive of hypertension diagnoses for airmen in their second YOS and older airmen, but run time is not statistically significant for older airmen when examining the other health outcomes. Table B.4 shows the results for all first and second years observed, across YOS.

Finally, we estimated the model exploring health diagnoses with ICD-10 codes, meaning that we examined diagnoses that occurred during or after FY 2016. As shown in Table B.5, the patterns are similar but slightly less robust than those seen earlier, likely because of smaller sample sizes used to detect the relatively small effects that we were able to observe in the larger earlier sample using ICD-9 codes. The relationship between the 1.5-mile run time is a statistically significant predictor of new other cardiovascular disease diagnoses as well as new overuse injuries and other musculoskeletal conditions. Push-up scores are also statistically significant predictors of new overuse injuries and other musculoskeletal conditions, based on the limited data available after the introduction of ICD-10.

Table B.2. Odds Ratios of the Effect of AF-FA Component Scores on New Diagnoses Two Years Later

AF-FA Component	Hypertension	Other Cardiovascular Disease	Diabetes	Overuse Injuries	Other Musculoskeletal Conditions
AC	1.033*	0.100	1.032*	0.990*	0.993*
	(0.006)	(0.003)	(0.013)	(0.002)	(0.002)
1.5-mile run	1.001	1.004	1.010	0.998	0.997
	(0.004)	(0.002)	(0.009)	(0.002)	(0.002)
Sit-ups	0.994*	1.002*	0.993*	1.004*	1.002*
	(0.002)	(0.001)	(0.003)	(0.001)	(0.001)
Push-ups	1.001	0.999	0.997	0.999	1.002*
	(0.001)	(0.001)	(0.003)	(0.000)	(0.001)
Demographic Variable					
Asian or Pacific Islander	1.168*	0.858*	1.638*	0.946**	0.962
	(0.069)	(0.026)	(0.187)	(0.020)	(0.022)
Black	1.545*	1.079*	1.451*	1.006	1.020
	(0.047)	(0.017)	(0.096)	(0.012)	(0.014)
Hispanic	0.871*	0.919*	1.434*	1.044*	1.034*
	(0.039)	(0.018)	(0.117)	(0.014)	(0.015)
Other race	1.073	0.966	1.390*	0.992	1.070*
	(0.085)	(0.037)	(0.218)	(0.029)	(0.033)
Enlisted	1.453*	1.228*	1.659*	1.316*	1.401*
	(0.049)	(0.021)	(0.129)	(0.017)	(0.020)
Ever deployed	0.748*	0.737*	0.627*	0.764*	0.726*
	(0.021)	(0.010)	(0.042)	(0.007)	(0.008)
Height	0.918*	0.973*	0.924*	0.992*	0.988*
	(0.005)	(0.002)	(0.010)	(0.002)	(0.002)
Weight	1.017*	1.008*	1.014*	1.005*	1.006*

AF-FA Component	Hypertension	Other Cardiovascular Disease	Diabetes	Overuse Injuries	Other Musculoskeletal Conditions
	(0.001)	(0.000)	(0.002)	(0.000)	(0.000)
Age	1.073*	1.020*	1.068*	1.015*	1.006*
	(0.004)	(0.002)	(0.009)	(0.002)	(0.002)
YOS	0.999	0.100	1.005	1.001	0.996*
	(0.004)	(0.002)	(0.008)	(0.002)	(0.002)
Female	0.851*	1.273*	1.837*	1.293*	1.212*
	(0.045)	(0.030)	(0.193)	(0.023)	(0.023)
Observations (n)	437,280	437,280	437,280	437,280	437,280
Y-mean	0.021	0.086	0.005	0.158	0.135

NOTE: The logistic regression model was estimated by using AF-FA component scores and demographic characteristics in the first year observed and new diagnoses in the third year observed. It includes airmen of all YOS and focuses on ICD-9 diagnoses (i.e., FY 2004–FY 2015). Scores for each AF-FA component are measured as follows: AC is measured in inches, run times in minutes, and sit-ups and push-ups in the number of each performed during 1-minute timed tests. Standard errors are shown in parentheses. * $p < 0.05$; **$p < 0.01$.

Table B.3. Odds Ratios of the Effect of AF-FA Component Scores on New Diagnoses in the Following Year, by Seniority

AF-FA Component	Hypertension		Other Cardiovascular Disease		Diabetes		Overuse Injuries		Other Musculoskeletal Conditions	
	YOS = 2	YOS > 2	YOS = 2	YOS > 2	YOS = 2	YOS > 2	YOS = 2	YOS > 2	YOS = 2	YOS > 2
AC	1.045*	1.063*	0.100	1.006	0.985	1.112*	0.990*	0.994	1.004	1.002
	(0.013)	(0.008)	(0.004)	(0.005)	(0.022)	(0.024)	(0.003)	(0.003)	(0.003)	(0.004)
1.5-mile run	1.054*	1.011*	1.041*	0.998	1.041	0.997	1.008*	0.100	1.010*	1.000
	(0.022)	(0.005)	(0.007)	(0.003)	(0.037)	(0.012)	(0.004)	(0.002)	(0.005)	(0.002)
Sit-ups	1.001	0.997	1.003*	0.999	0.996	0.984*	1.002*	1.001	1.005*	1.001
	(0.004)	(0.002)	(0.001)	(0.001)	(0.007)	(0.005)	(0.001)	(0.001)	(0.001)	(0.001)
Push-ups	1.006*	0.999	1.002	1.000	0.993	0.100	1.001	1.001*	1.002*	1.003*
	(0.003)	(0.002)	(0.001)	(0.001)	(0.005)	(0.004)	(0.001)	(0.001)	(0.001)	(0.001)
Demographic Variable										
Asian or Pacific Islander	0.961	1.520*	0.779*	0.918	1.289	1.750*	0.909*	0.950	0.994	1.023
	(0.108)	(0.117)	(0.031)	(0.046)	(0.247)	(0.324)	(0.024)	(0.034)	(0.027)	(0.038)
Black	1.551*	1.572*	1.124*	1.129*	1.446*	1.779*	1.031*	1.012	1.072*	0.988
	(0.091)	(0.064)	(0.024)	(0.029)	(0.176)	(0.187)	(0.016)	(0.019)	(0.017)	(0.021)
Hispanic	0.694*	0.960	0.886*	0.972	1.262	1.416*	1.039**	1.057**	1.054*	1.033
	(0.054)	(0.063)	(0.020)	(0.035)	(0.161)	(0.207)	(0.016)	(0.027)	(0.017)	(0.028)
Other race	1.415*	1.092	0.903	1.024	1.487	1.725*	1.039	1.063	1.017	1.019
	(0.180)	(0.114)	(0.049)	(0.060)	(0.385)	(0.389)	(0.038)	(0.045)	(0.040)	(0.047)
White (omitted)										
Enlisted	1.556*	1.354*	1.370*	1.138*	1.453*	1.388*	1.629*	1.271*	1.820*	1.346*
	(0.117)	(0.057)	(0.037)	(0.028)	(0.221)	(0.150)	(0.032)	(0.023)	(0.039)	(0.027)
Ever deployed	0.793*	0.800*	0.664*	0.778*	0.600*	0.617*	0.624*	0.801*	0.624*	0.770*

AF-FA Component	Hypertension		Other Cardiovascular Disease		Diabetes		Overuse Injuries		Other Musculoskeletal Conditions	
	YOS = 2	YOS > 2	YOS = 2	YOS > 2	YOS = 2	YOS > 2	YOS = 2	YOS > 2	YOS = 2	YOS > 2
	(0.048)	(0.033)	(0.014)	(0.018)	(0.084)	(0.075)	(0.010)	(0.014)	(0.010)	(0.014)
Height	0.938*	0.930*	0.978*	0.979*	0.945*	0.908*	0.987*	0.993**	0.993*	0.999*
	(0.009)	(0.006)	(0.003)	(0.004)	(0.019)	(0.016)	(0.002)	(0.003)	(0.002)	(0.003)
Weight	1.021*	1.013*	1.009*	1.007*	1.009*	1.006*	1.007*	1.005*	1.007*	1.005*
	(0.001)	(0.001)	(0.000)	(0.001)	(0.003)	(0.003)	(0.000)	(0.000)	(0.000)	(0.000)
Age	1.099*	1.067*	1.020*	1.031*	1.071*	1.095*	1.026*	1.014*	1.012*	1.002
	(0.008)	(0.006)	(0.003)	(0.003)	(0.019)	(0.014)	(0.002)	(0.002)	(0.002)	(0.003)
YOS	1.087	1.005	0.967*	0.996	1.211*	0.994	0.936*	1.006**	0.904*	0.999
	(0.050)	(0.005)	(0.015)	(0.003)	(0.111)	(0.013)	(0.010)	(0.003)	(0.010)	(0.003)
Female	1.212	0.888	1.493*	1.301*	1.805*	1.218	1.552*	1.359*	1.316*	1.256*
	(0.123)	(0.065)	(0.047)	(0.051)	(0.329)	(0.215)	(0.035)	(0.039)	(0.031)	(0.039)
Observations (n)	274,392	175,389	274,392	175,389	274,392	175,389	274,392	175,389	274,392	175,389
Y-mean	0.008	0.023	0.073	0.080	0.002	0.004	0.158	0.157	0.145	0.135

NOTE: The logistic regression model was estimated by using AF-FA component scores and demographic characteristics in the first year observed and new diagnoses in the second year observed. It focuses on ICD-9 diagnoses (i.e., FY 2004–FY 2015). Scores for each AF-FA component are measured as follows: AC is measured in inches, run times in minutes, and sit-ups and push-ups in the number of each performed during 1-minute timed tests. Standard errors are shown in parentheses. $* p < 0.05$; $** p < 0.01$.

Table B.4. Odds Ratios of the Effect of AF-FA Component Scores on New Diagnoses in the Following Year

AF-FA Component	Hypertension	Other Cardiovascular Disease	Diabetes	Overuse Injuries	Other Musculoskeletal Conditions
AC	1.055*	0.998	1.055*	0.989*	0.999
	(0.007)	(0.003)	(0.016)	(0.002)	(0.002)
1.5-mile run	1.014*	1.005*	1.003	1.002	1.000
	(0.005)	(0.003)	(0.010)	(0.002)	(0.002)
Sit-ups	0.997	1.003*	0.992	1.003*	1.004*
	(0.002)	(0.001)	(0.004)	(0.001)	(0.001)
Push-ups	1.001	0.100	0.996	1.001	1.002*
	(0.001)	(0.001)	(0.003)	(0.000)	(0.001)
Demographic Variable					
Asian or Pacific Islander	1.289*	0.823*	1.491*	0.918*	0.997
	(0.081)	(0.026)	(0.199)	(0.019)	(0.022)
Black	1.553*	1.118*	1.593*	1.016	1.034*
	(0.052)	(0.018)	(0.126)	(0.012)	(0.013)
Hispanic	0.823*	0.917*	1.360*	1.051*	1.052*
	(0.041)	(0.018)	(0.130)	(0.014)	(0.015)
Other race	1.210*	0.938	1.584*	1.040	1.010
	(0.098)	(0.037)	(0.268)	(0.029)	(0.030)
White (omitted)					
Enlisted	1.385*	1.252*	1.443*	1.449*	1.588*
	(0.051)	(0.022)	(0.124)	(0.019)	(0.023)
Ever deployed	0.805*	0.706*	0.596*	0.691*	0.676*
	(0.027)	(0.011)	(0.054)	(0.008)	(0.008)
Height	0.930*	0.977*	0.919*	0.989*	0.992*
	(0.005)	(0.002)	(0.012)	(0.002)	(0.002)
Weight	1.016*	1.008*	1.008*	1.006*	1.006*
	(0.001)	(0.000)	(0.002)	(0.000)	(0.000)
Age	1.079*	1.027*	1.082*	1.022*	1.011*
	(0.004)	(0.002)	(0.011)	(0.002)	(0.002)
YOS	0.996	0.990*	0.985	0.992*	0.987*
	(0.004)	(0.002)	(0.010)	(0.002)	(0.002)
Female	0.999	1.444*	1.539*	1.477*	1.285*
	(0.058)	(0.034)	(0.184)	(0.025)	(0.024)
Observations (*n*)	449,781	449,781	449,781	449,781	449,781
Y-mean	0.018	0.079	0.003	0.160	0.141

NOTE: The logistic regression model was estimated by using AF-FA component scores and demographic characteristics in the first year observed and new diagnoses in the second year observed. It includes airmen in all YOS and focuses on ICD-9 diagnoses (i.e., FY 2004–FY 2015). Scores for each AF-FA component are measured as follows: AC is measured in inches, run times in minutes, and sit-ups and push-ups in the number of each performed during 1-minute timed tests. Standard errors are shown in parentheses. * $p < 0.05$, ** $p < 0.01$.

Table B.5. Odds Ratios of the Effect of AF-FA Component Scores on New Diagnoses in the Following Year

AF-FA Component	Hypertension	Other Cardiovascular Disease	Diabetes	Overuse Injuries	Other Musculoskeletal Conditions
AC	1.029	0.988	1.018	0.998	0.995
	(0.034)	(0.008)	(0.053)	(0.005)	(0.007)
1.5-mile run	1.046	1.074*	0.952	1.033*	1.020
	(0.052)	(0.014)	(0.063)	(0.009)	(0.012)
Sit-ups	1.000	1.001	1.000	0.100	1.003
	(0.008)	(0.002)	(0.014)	(0.001)	(0.002)
Push-ups	0.998	1.002	0.988	1.005*	1.004*
	(0.005)	(0.001)	(0.010)	(0.001)	(0.001)
Demographic Variable					
Asian or Pacific Islander	1.019	0.851*	1.334	1.008	1.054
	(0.214)	(0.048)	(0.469)	(0.035)	(0.049)
Black	1.719*	1.057	2.638*	1.026	1.118*
	(0.220)	(0.039)	(0.574)	(0.025)	(0.036)
Hispanic	0.762	0.957	1.416	1.020	1.028
	(0.128)	(0.035)	(0.332)	(0.024)	(0.032)
Other race	1.652	0.855	0.403	0.968	1.018
	(0.467)	(0.091)	(0.406)	(0.063)	(0.088)
White (omitted)					
Enlisted	1.085	1.378*	0.758	1.470*	1.573*
	(0.162)	(0.065)	(0.206)	(0.044)	(0.064)
Ever deployed	0.671*	0.625*	0.827	0.680*	0.622*
	(0.123)	(0.030)	(0.242)	(0.020)	(0.025)
Height	0.942*	0.984*	0.902*	0.983*	0.991*
	(0.023)	(0.006)	(0.035)	(0.004)	(0.005)
Weight	1.017*	1.006*	1.014*	1.009*	1.008*
	(0.003)	(0.001)	(0.006)	(0.001)	(0.001)
Age	1.083*	1.007	1.055*	1.012*	1.011*
	(0.013)	(0.004)	(0.023)	(0.003)	(0.004)
YOS	1.011	1.046*	1.034	1.003	1.022
	(0.031)	(0.013)	(0.049)	(0.011)	(0.014)
Female	0.909	1.325*	1.789	1.690*	1.469*
	(0.197)	(0.075)	(0.581)	(0.061)	(0.071)
Observations	81,993	81,993	81,993	81,993	81,993
Y-mean	0.006	0.087	0.002	0.237	0.120

NOTE: The logistic regression model was estimated by using AF-FA component scores and demographic characteristics in the second year observed and new diagnoses in the third year observed. It includes airmen in all YOS and focuses on ICD-10 diagnoses (i.e., FY 2016–FY 2019). Scores for each AF-FA component are measured as follows: AC is measured in inches, run times in minutes, and sit-ups and push-ups in the number of each performed during 1-minute timed tests. Standard errors are shown in parentheses. * $p < 0.05$

Detailed Survival Analyses Results

We also performed survival analyses to consider the relationship between fitness and health outcomes, such as diabetes, other cardiovascular disease (beyond hypertension), and other musculoskeletal conditions. We found the overall pattern to be that airmen in the moderate- or high-risk categories for AC fitness have the highest hazards of each of the adverse health outcomes, when controlling for other fitness component levels. Moderate or high risk for aerobic fitness (assessed by the 1.5-mile run) is related to higher risks of adverse health outcomes, but to a lesser extent than AC fitness, when controlling for other fitness component levels. In most cases, being in a higher-risk fitness category for push-ups or sit-ups is either not significantly related to a higher risk of health and injury diagnoses, when controlling for other fitness component levels, or the relative increase in risk is small (less than 10 percent). All hazard ratio results for each health outcome are shown in Table B.6.

Table B.6. Estimated Hazard Ratios of Adverse Health Outcomes, by Diagnosis Type, Fitness Category, and Gender

AF-FA Component	Fitness Category	Estimated Hazard Ratio for Diagnosis (Relative to the Low-Risk Fitness Category)		
		All Airmen	Female Airmen	Male Airmen
Diabetes				
AC	Moderate risk	1.86 [1.80, 1.91]	1.85 [1.74, 1.97]	1.85 [1.79, 1.92]
	High risk	3.53 [3.35, 3.73]	4.19 [3.66, 4.79]	3.41 [3.21, 3.62]
1.5-mile run	Moderate risk	1.40 [1.35, 1.44]	1.23 [1.15, 1.32]	1.45 [1.40, 1.51]
	High risk	1.94 [1.85, 2.04]	0.93 [0.67, 1.28]	2.01 [1.91, 2.12]
Push-ups	Moderate risk	1.04 [1.00, 1.08]	1.06 [0.99, 1.13]	1.02 [0.97, 1.07]
	High risk	1.02 [0.96, 1.08]	1.04 [0.96, 1.14]	1.03 [0.95, 1.12]
Sit-ups	Moderate risk	1.20 [1.15, 1.24]	1.08 [0.99, 1.17]	1.23 [1.18, 1.29]
	High risk	1.38 [1.31, 1.45]	1.15 [1.04, 1.28]	1.46 [1.38, 1.55]
Hypertension				
AC	Moderate risk	2.01 [1.97, 2.04]	1.78 [1.70, 1.87]	2.05 [2.01, 2.09]
	High risk	3.25 [3.16, 3.35]	3.27 [2.95, 3.62]	3.27 [3.16, 3.37]
1.5-mile run	Moderate risk	1.35 [1.32, 1.38]	1.22 [1.15, 1.28]	1.37 [1.34, 1.40]
	High risk	1.85 [1.81, 1.90]	1.23 [0.99, 1.55]	1.87 [1.82, 1.92]
Push-ups	Moderate risk	0.98 [0.96, 1.01]	1.06 [1.00, 1.11]	0.97 [0.95, 0.99]
	High risk	1.00 [0.97, 1.03]	1.06 [0.99, 1.13]	0.99 [0.95, 1.03]
Sit-ups	Moderate risk	1.16 [1.13, 1.18]	1.17 [1.10, 1.24]	1.16 [1.13, 1.19]
	High risk	1.30 [1.27, 1.34]	1.24 [1.14, 1.34]	1.32 [1.28, 1.36]
Other cardiovascular diagnoses				
AC	Moderate risk	1.34 [1.32, 1.35]	1.14 [1.11, 1.16]	1.39 [1.37, 1.40]
	High risk	1.74 [1.71, 1.78]	1.50 [1.41, 1.60]	1.79 [1.75, 1.83]
1.5-mile run	Moderate risk	1.12 [1.11, 1.13]	1.05 [1.03, 1.08]	1.14 [1.12, 1.15]
	High risk	1.42 [1.40, 1.44]	1.12 [1.03, 1.21]	1.43 [1.40, 1.45]
Push-ups	Moderate risk	1.03 [1.02, 1.04]	1.07 [1.05, 1.09]	1.01 [1.00, 1.02]
	High risk	1.05 [1.03, 1.06]	1.08 [1.05, 1.11]	1.05 [1.03, 1.07]
Sit-ups	Moderate risk	1.05 [1.04, 1.06]	1.04 [1.01, 1.06]	1.05 [1.04, 1.07]
	High risk	1.08 [1.07, 1.10]	1.02 [0.99, 1.06]	1.11 [1.09, 1.13]

AF-FA Component	Fitness Category	Estimated Hazard Ratio for Diagnosis (Relative to the Low-Risk Fitness Category)		
		All Airmen	Female Airmen	Male Airmen
Overuse injuries				
AC	Moderate risk	1.19 [1.18, 1.19]	1.15 [1.13, 1.17]	1.19 [1.18, 1.20]
	High risk	1.48 [1.45, 1.51]	1.50 [1.42, 1.58]	1.48 [1.45, 1.51]
1.5-mile run	Moderate risk	1.04 [1.03, 1.05]	1.01 [0.99, 1.03]	1.05 [1.04, 1.06]
	High risk	1.25 [1.24, 1.27]	1.03 [0.96, 1.10]	1.26 [1.25, 1.28]
Push-ups	Moderate risk	1.03 [1.02, 1.03]	1.08 [1.06, 1.10]	1.01 [1.00, 1.02]
	High risk	1.08 [1.06, 1.09]	1.08 [1.06, 1.11]	1.09 [1.07, 1.11]
Sit-ups	Moderate risk	0.99 [0.98, 1.00]	1.00 [0.98, 1.02]	0.99 [0.98, 1.00]
	High risk	1.00 [0.99, 1.01]	0.94 [0.92, 0.97]	1.02 [1.01, 1.04]
Other musculoskeletal injuries				
AC	Moderate risk	1.22 [1.21, 1.23]	1.20 [1.18, 1.23]	1.22 [1.21, 1.23]
	High risk	1.49 [1.46, 1.52]	1.64 [1.55, 1.72]	1.47 [1.44, 1.50]
1.5-mile run	Moderate risk	1.01 [1.00, 1.02]	1.00 [0.98, 1.03]	1.01 [1.00, 1.02]
	High risk	1.20 [1.18, 1.22]	1.04 [0.96, 1.11]	1.21 [1.19, 1.22]
Push-ups	Moderate risk	1.00 [0.99, 1.01]	1.07 [1.05, 1.09]	0.98 [0.97, 0.99]
	High risk	1.03 [1.02, 1.04]	1.06 [1.03, 1.08]	1.03 [1.01, 1.05]
Sit-ups	Moderate risk	0.97 [0.96, 0.97]	0.98 [0.96, 1.00]	0.96 [0.95, 0.97]
	High risk	0.97 [0.96, 0.99]	0.91 [0.89, 0.94]	1.00 [0.98, 1.01]

NOTE: For each of the four fitness components, we adapted low-, moderate-, or high-risk fitness categories based on the AF fitness scoring system (AFI 36-2905, 2020). Values shown are the estimated hazard ratios (e.g., 1.86 times greater risk) for airmen of receiving diagnoses over the course of their careers if their fitness falls into the moderate- or high-risk categories (relative to those with fitness in the low-risk category). Hazard ratios are estimated controlling for all fitness categories and individual demographics. Values in parenthesis show 95-percent confidence intervals for the estimates.

We also found that lower-incidence health outcomes, such as diabetes or hypertension, have higher hazard ratios for airmen in higher risk fitness categories. This generally makes sense, because the majority of airmen are likely to receive common diagnoses regardless of their fitness, such as overuse injuries which have an estimated incidence of 58 percent of airmen within their first four YOS. On the other hand, increases of a few percentage points in rare diagnoses, such as diabetes (with an estimated incidence of 1.63 percent of airmen within their first four YOS), can result in high hazard ratios. Table B.6 shows that airmen in the high-risk fitness category for AC are 3.5 times more likely to receive a diabetes diagnosis than airmen in the low-risk category, while they are only 1.5 times more likely to receive an overuse injuries diagnosis.

Figure B.1 shows the overall estimated survival over time for hypertension, by fitness category, for the AC and the 1.5-mile run components, based on an airman's initial FA scores;

Figure B.2 shows other cardiovascular outcomes; Figure B.3 shows diabetes; Figure B.4 shows overuse injuries; and Figure B.5 shows other musculoskeletal injuries.

Figure B.1. Estimated Survival over Time for Hypertension Based on Abdominal Circumference and 1.5-Mile Run Initial Fitness Scores, by Fitness Category

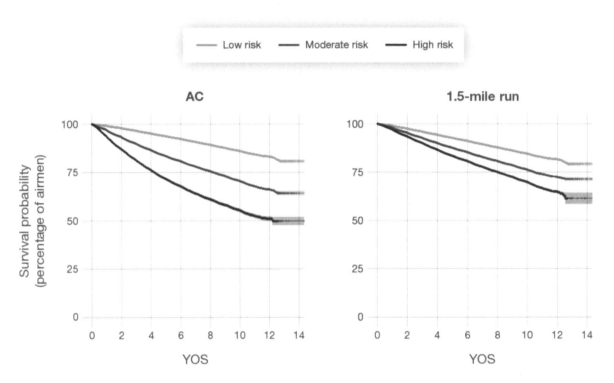

NOTE: For the survival analyses, we adapted low-, moderate-, and high-risk fitness categories based on the AF-FA scoring system (AFI 36-2905, 2020) for each of the four AF-FA components. Fitness scores for AC and cardiorespiratory endurance (i.e., the 1.5-mile run) are determined by AF standards, which we used to generate cutoffs for approximately equivalent fitness categories for push-ups and sit-ups. For AC, standards vary by gender, and for the 1.5-mile run, standards vary by gender and age. Plots show the estimated percentages of airmen in each fitness category (based on their first-year FA scores) who would not be likely to receive a hypertension diagnosis by the YOS shown.

Figure B.2. Estimated Survival over Time for Other Cardiovascular Disease Based on Abdominal Circumference and 1.5-Mile Run Initial Fitness Scores, by Fitness Category

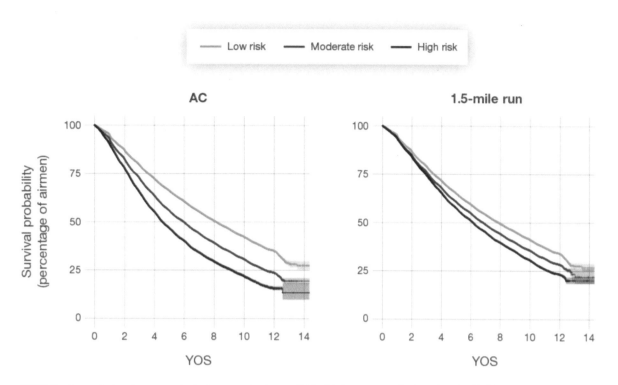

NOTE: For the survival analyses, we adapted low-, moderate-, and high-risk fitness categories based on the AF-FA scoring system (AFI 36-2905, 2020) for each of the four AF-FA components. Fitness scores for AC and cardiorespiratory endurance (i.e., the 1.5-mile run) are determined by AF standards, which we used to generate cutoffs for approximately equivalent fitness categories for push-ups and sit-ups. For AC, standards vary by gender, and for the 1.5-mile run, standards vary by gender and age. Plots show the estimated percentages of female and male airmen, respectively, in each fitness category (based on their first-year FA scores) who would not be likely to receive a diagnosis for other cardiovascular disease by the YOS shown.

Figure B.3. Estimated Survival over Time for Diabetes Based on Abdominal Circumference and 1.5-Mile Run Initial Fitness Scores, by Fitness Category

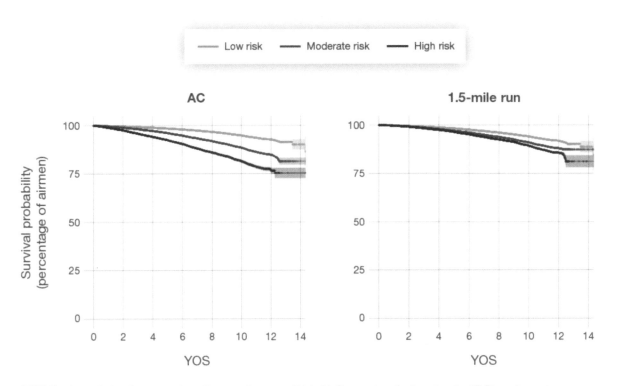

NOTE: For the survival analyses, we adapted low-, moderate-, and high-risk fitness categories based on the AF-FA scoring system (AFI 36-2905, 2020) for each of the four AF-FA components. Fitness scores for AC and cardiorespiratory endurance (i.e., the 1.5-mile run) are determined by AF standards, which we used to generate cutoffs for approximately equivalent fitness categories for push-ups and sit-ups. For AC, standards vary by gender, and for the 1.5-mile run, standards vary by gender and age. Plots show the estimated percentages of female and male airmen, respectively, in each fitness category (based on their first-year FA scores) who would not be likely to receive a diabetes diagnosis by the YOS shown.

Figure B.4. Estimated Survival over Time for Overuse Injuries Based on Abdominal Circumference and 1.5-Mile Run Initial Fitness Scores, by Fitness Category

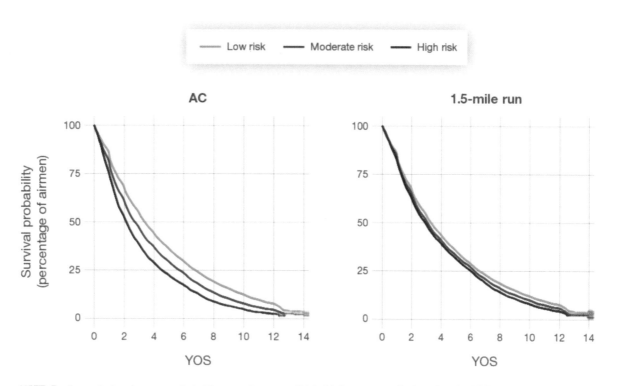

NOTE: For the survival analyses, we adapted low-, moderate-, and high-risk fitness categories based on the AF-FA scoring system (AFI 36-2905, 2020) for each of the four AF-FA components. Fitness scores for AC and cardiorespiratory endurance (i.e., the 1.5-mile run) are determined by AF standards, which we used to generate cutoffs for approximately equivalent fitness categories for push-ups and sit-ups. For AC, standards vary by gender, and for the 1.5-mile run, standards vary by gender and age. Plots show the estimated percentages of female and male airmen, respectively, in each fitness category (based on their first-year FA scores) who would not be likely to receive an overuse injuries diagnosis by the YOS shown.

Figure B.5. Estimated Survival over Time for Other Musculoskeletal Conditions Based on Abdominal Circumference and 1.5-Mile Run Initial Fitness Scores, by Fitness Category

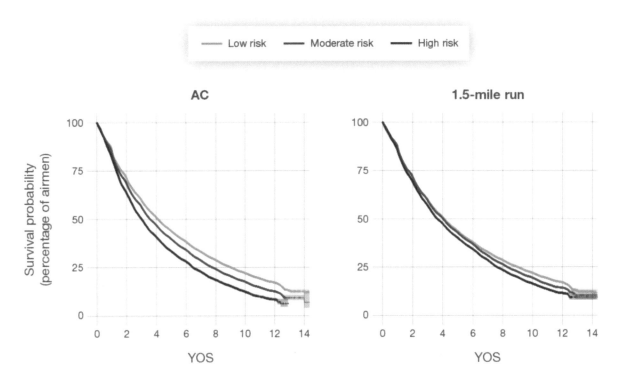

NOTE: For the survival analyses, we adapted low-, moderate-, and high-risk fitness categories based on the AF-FA scoring system (AFI 36-2905, 2020) for each of the four AF-FA components. Fitness scores for AC and cardiorespiratory endurance (i.e., the 1.5-mile run) are determined by AF standards, which we used to generate cutoffs for approximately equivalent fitness categories for push-ups and sit-ups. For AC, standards vary by gender, and for the 1.5-mile run, standards vary by gender and age. Plots show the estimated percentages of female and male airmen, respectively, in each fitness category (based on their first-year FA scores) who would not be likely to receive an other musculoskeletal conditions diagnosis by the YOS shown.

We also estimated prevalence and hazard ratios separately for female and male airmen, and we looked at hazard ratios separately by race. These results are shown in Figures B.6 through B.10 and in Tables B.7 through B.9. We found that, overall, female airmen had higher estimated incidences of diabetes, other cardiovascular disease, overuse injuries, and other musculoskeletal conditions than male airmen, while male airmen, overall, had a higher estimated incidence of hypertension than female airmen. We found that poor AC fitness is related to the highest likelihood of adverse health outcomes for both female and male airmen, in the same way it was for all airmen combined. For most health outcomes, we found that poor fitness on the 1.5-mile run and sit-ups components is related to higher rates of adverse health outcomes for male airmen compared with female airmen, while poor fitness on push-ups is more frequently related to higher adverse outcomes for female airmen. It is possible that these results would change using different cutoffs for the fitness risk categories,[43] but based on the current AF fitness points

---

[43] We found, for example, that very few female airmen are in the high-risk category for the 1.5-mile run, which might be because of the higher run time cutoffs for that gender, but further research is needed to determine whether using different cutoffs would substantially alter our findings.

system, it appears that there are somewhat different health risks associated with similar AF-defined levels of fitness between male and female airmen.

Figure B.6. Estimated Survival over Time for Hypertension Based on Abdominal Circumference and 1.5-Mile Run Initial Fitness Scores, by Gender

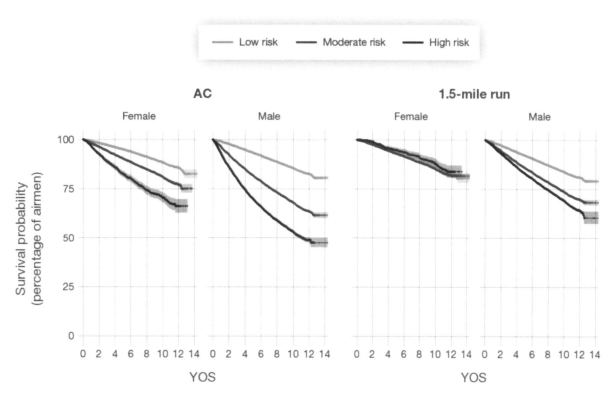

NOTE: For the survival analyses, we adapted low-, moderate-, and high-risk fitness categories based on the AF-FA scoring system (AFI 36-2905, 2020) for each of the four AF-FA components. Fitness scores for AC and cardiorespiratory endurance (i.e., the 1.5-mile run) are determined by AF standards, which we used to generate cutoffs for approximately equivalent fitness categories for push-ups and sit-ups. For AC, standards vary by gender, and for the 1.5-mile run, standards vary by gender and age. Plots show the estimated percentages of female and male airmen, respectively, in each fitness category (based on their first-year FA scores) who would not be likely to receive a hypertension diagnosis by the YOS shown.

Figure B.7. Estimated Survival over Time for Other Cardiovascular Disease Based on Abdominal Circumference and 1.5-Mile Run Initial Fitness Scores, by Gender

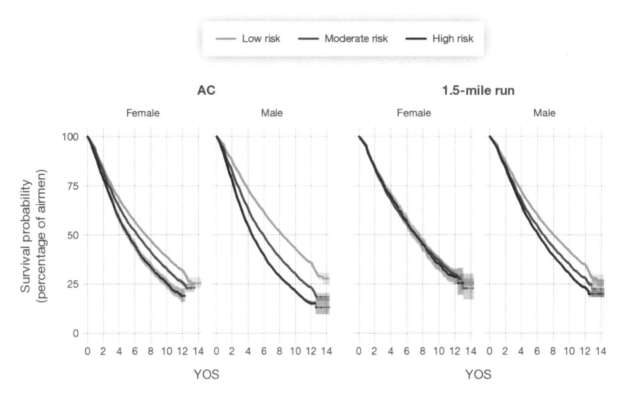

NOTE: For the survival analyses, we adapted low-, moderate-, and high-risk fitness categories based on the AF-FA scoring system (AFI 36-2905, 2020) for each of the four AF-FA components. Fitness scores for AC and cardiorespiratory endurance (i.e., the 1.5-mile run) are determined by AF standards, which we used to generate cutoffs for approximately equivalent fitness categories for push-ups and sit-ups. For AC, standards vary by gender, and for the 1.5-mile run, standards vary by gender and age. Plots show the estimated percentages of female and male airmen, respectively, in each fitness category (based on their first-year FA scores) who would not be likely to receive a diagnosis for other cardiovascular disease by the YOS shown.

Figure B.8. Estimated Survival over Time for Diabetes Based on Abdominal Circumference and 1.5-Mile Run Initial Fitness Scores, by Gender

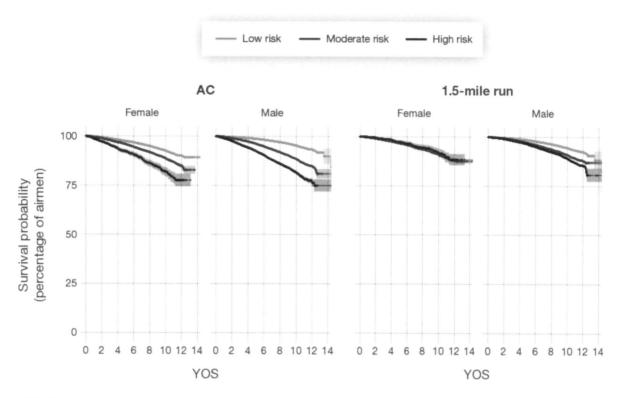

NOTE: For the survival analyses, we adapted low-, moderate-, and high-risk fitness categories based on the AF-FA scoring system (AFI 36-2905, 2020) for each of the four AF-FA components. Fitness scores for AC and cardiorespiratory endurance (i.e., the 1.5-mile run) are determined by AF standards, which we used to generate cutoffs for approximately equivalent fitness categories for push-ups and sit-ups. For AC, standards vary by gender, and for the 1.5-mile run, standards vary by gender and age. Plots show the estimated percentages of female and male airmen, respectively, in each fitness category (based on their first-year FA scores) who would not be likely to receive a diabetes diagnosis by the YOS shown.

Figure B.9. Estimated Survival over Time for Overuse Injuries Based on Abdominal Circumference and 1.5-Mile Run Initial Fitness Scores, by Gender

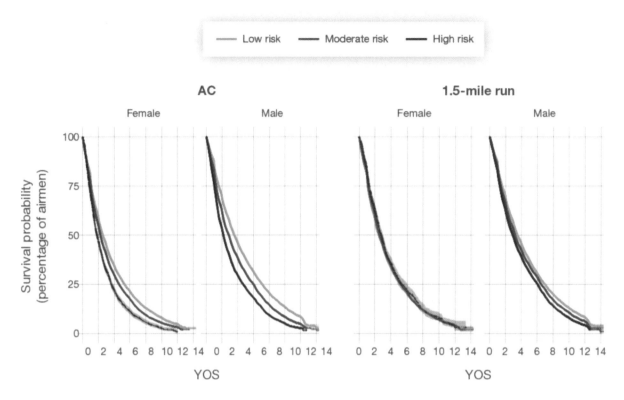

NOTE: For the survival analyses, we adapted low-, moderate-, and high-risk fitness categories based on the AF-FA scoring system (AFI 36-2905, 2020) for each of the four AF-FA components. Fitness scores for AC and cardiorespiratory endurance (i.e., the 1.5-mile run) are determined by AF standards, which we used to generate cutoffs for approximately equivalent fitness categories for push-ups and sit-ups. For AC, standards vary by gender, and for the 1.5-mile run, standards vary by gender and age. Plots show the estimated percentages of female and male airmen, respectively, in each fitness category (based on their first-year FA scores) who would not be likely to receive an overuse injuries diagnosis by the YOS shown.

Figure B.10. Estimated Survival over Time for Other Musculoskeletal Conditions Based on Abdominal Circumference and 1.5-Mile Run Initial Fitness Scores, by Gender

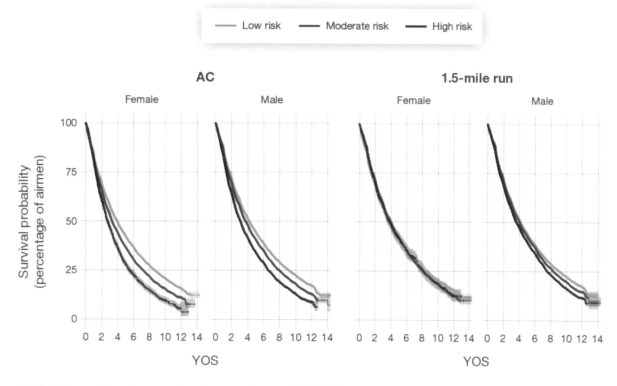

NOTE: For the survival analyses, we adapted low-, moderate-, and high-risk fitness categories based on the AF-FA scoring system (AFI 36-2905, 2020) for each of the four AF-FA components. Fitness scores for AC and cardiorespiratory endurance (i.e., the 1.5-mile run) are determined by AF standards, which we used to generate cutoffs for approximately equivalent fitness categories for push-ups and sit-ups. For AC, standards vary by gender, and for the 1.5-mile run, standards vary by gender and age. Plots show the estimated percentages of female and male airmen, respectively, in each fitness category (based on their first-year FA scores) who would not be likely to receive an other musculoskeletal diagnosis by the YOS shown.

Table B.7. Estimated Incidence of Health Outcomes, by Diagnosis Type, Fitness Category, and Gender

AF-FA Component	AF-FA Fitness Category	Estimated Percentage of Diagnosis Within First Four Years of Service		
		All Airmen	Female Airmen	Male Airmen
Diabetes				
Overall incidence	All	1.63% [1.60, 1.67]	2.33% [2.22, 2.43]	1.46% [1.42, 1.50]
AC	Low risk	1.08% [1.04, 1.11]	1.86% [1.75, 1.96]	0.89% [0.86, 0.92]
	Moderate risk	2.73% [2.63, 2.84]	3.13% [2.88, 3.38]	2.63% [2.51, 2.75]
	High risk	5.81% [5.47, 6.14]	6.27% [5.30, 7.23]	5.73% [5.37, 6.09]
1.5-mile run	Low risk	1.25% [1.22, 1.29]	2.04% [1.94, 2.15]	1.05% [1.01, 1.09]
	Moderate risk	2.11% [1.99, 2.22]	2.37% [2.11, 2.63]	2.03% [1.90, 2.16]
	High risk	2.50% [2.34, 2.66]	1.76% [0.96, 2.55]	2.53% [2.36, 2.69]

AF-FA Component	AF-FA Fitness Category	Estimated Percentage of Diagnosis Within First Four Years of Service		
		All Airmen	Female Airmen	Male Airmen
Push-ups	Low risk	1.44% [1.39, 1.48]	1.73% [1.59, 1.87]	1.39% [1.34, 1.44]
	Moderate risk	1.53% [1.46, 1.59]	2.30% [2.15, 2.46]	1.28% [1.21, 1.35]
	High risk	2.09% [1.97, 2.21]	2.69% [2.46, 2.92]	1.75% [1.61, 1.89]
Sit-ups	Low risk	1.28% [1.24, 1.32]	1.99% [1.87, 2.10]	1.12% [1.08, 1.16]
	Moderate risk	1.81% [1.72, 1.90]	2.41% [2.18, 2.64]	1.66% [1.56, 1.75]
	High risk	2.51% [2.38, 2.63]	2.74% [2.45, 3.02]	2.45% [2.31, 2.59]
Hypertension				
Overall incidence	All	7.36% [7.28, 7.43]	5.06% [4.92, 5.20]	7.92% [7.83, 8.00]
AC	Low risk	4.83% [4.76, 4.90]	3.83% [3.69, 3.97]	5.07% [4.99, 5.15]
	Moderate risk	13.4% [13.2, 13.6]	7.64% [7.26, 8.01]	14.9% [14.6, 15.1]
	High risk	23.9% [23.3, 24.5]	14.2% [12.8, 15.5]	25.4% [24.7, 26.1]
1.5-mile run	Low risk	5.65% [5.57, 5.72]	4.28% [4.13, 4.42]	6.00% [5.91, 6.08]
	Moderate risk	9.99% [9.75, 10.2]	5.49% [5.10, 5.88]	11.3% [11.0, 11.6]
	High risk	13.4% [13.0, 13.7]	4.3% [3.06, 5.52]	13.3% [13.3, 14.0]
Push-ups	Low risk	7.17% [7.07, 7.27]	3.49% [3.30, 3.68]	7.74% [7.63, 7.85]
	Moderate risk	6.35% [6.22, 6.47]	4.92% [4.70, 5.15]	6.80% [6.66, 6.95]
	High risk	8.15% [7.92, 8.34]	6.13% [5.79, 6.47]	9.28% [8.97, 9.59]
Sit-ups	Low risk	5.96% [5.88, 6.04]	4.31% [4.15, 4.47]	6.34% [6.25, 6.44]
	Moderate risk	8.25% [8.06, 8.43]	5.22% [4.89, 5.55]	9.04% [8.82, 9.25]
	High risk	11.0% [10.8, 11.3]	5.70% [5.30, 6.10]	12.4% [12.1, 12.7]
Other cardiovascular disease				
Overall incidence	All	30.2% [30.1, 30.3]	33.0% [32.7, 33.3]	29.5% [29.4, 29.7]
AC	Low risk	27.6% [27.5, 27.8]	31.4% [31.1, 31.8]	26.7% [26.5, 26.9]
	Moderate risk	36.4% [36.0, 36.7]	35.6% [34.9, 36.2]	36.5% [36.2, 36.9]
	High risk	44.8% [44.0, 45.5]	41.6% [41.6, 43.6]	45.2% [44.4, 46.0]
1.5-mile run	Low risk	28.4% [28.3, 28.6]	31.7% [31.3, 32.0]	27.6% [27.5, 27.8]
	Moderate risk	32.1% [31.7, 32.5]	32.1% [31.3, 32.9]	32.1% [31.7, 32.5]
	High risk	34.7% [34.2, 35.2]	30.3% [27.5, 33.0]	34.8% [34.3, 35.3]
Push-ups	Low risk	29.1% [28.9, 29.3]	29.9% [29.5, 30.4]	29.0% [28.8, 29.2]
	Moderate risk	29.9% [29.6, 30.1]	33.3% [32.8, 33.8]	28.8% [28.5, 29.1]
	High risk	32.0% [31.6, 32.4]	33.7% [33.0, 34.4]	31.1% [30.6, 31.6]
Sit-ups	Low risk	28.8% [28.6, 28.9]	32.0% [31.6, 32.3]	28.0% [27.8, 28.2]
	Moderate risk	31.1% [30.8, 31.5]	32.9% [32.2, 33.6]	30.7% [30.3, 31.0]
	High risk	32.9% [32.5, 33.2]	32.3% [31.5, 33.2]	33.0% [32.6, 33.4]
Overuse injuries				
Overall incidence	All	58.0% [57.9, 58.2]	67.1% [66.8, 67.4]	55.9% [55.8, 56.1]

AF-FA Component	AF-FA Fitness Category	Estimated Percentage of Diagnosis Within First Four Years of Service		
		All Airmen	Female Airmen	Male Airmen
AC	Low risk	55.9% [55.7, 56.0]	65.3% [65.0, 65.7]	53.7% [53.5, 53.9]
	Moderate risk	63.0% [62.7, 63.3]	70.1% [69.3, 70.8]	61.3% [60.9, 61.7]
	High risk	71.1% [70.4, 71.8]	77.9% [75.9, 79.7]	70.2% [69.4, 71.0]
1.5-mile run	Low risk	56.6% [56.4, 56.7]	66.1% [65.8, 66.5]	54.2% [54.1, 54.4]
	Moderate risk	59.3% [58.9, 59.7]	65.2% [64.3, 66.1]	57.7% [57.2, 58.2]
	High risk	61.0% [60.5, 61.5]	64.2% [60.9, 67.2]	60.9% [60.4, 61.4]
Push-ups	Low risk	56.5% [56.3, 56.7]	63.9% [63.4, 64.5]	55.4% [55.1, 55.6]
	Moderate risk	57.8% [57.6, 58.1]	67.9% [67.4, 68.4]	54.8% [54.5, 55.1]
	High risk	61.5% [61.1, 61.9]	67.3% [66.6, 68.0]	58.5% [58.0, 59.1]
Sit-ups	Low risk	56.7% [56.5, 56.9]	66.2% [65.8, 66.6]	54.6% [54.4, 54.8]
	Moderate risk	59.0% [58.6, 59.3]	67.1% [66.3, 67.8]	56.9% [56.6, 57.3]
	High risk	59.7% [59.3, 60.1]	65.7% [64.8, 66.6]	58.3% [57.8, 58.7]
Other musculoskeletal conditions				
Overall incidence	All	50.3% [50.1, 50.4]	52.5% [52.2, 52.9]	49.7% [49.6, 49.9]
AC	Low risk	48.9% [48.7, 49.0]	50.7% [50.3, 51.1]	48.4% [48.3, 48.6]
	Moderate risk	52.9% [52.6, 53.2]	56.0% [55.3, 56.8]	52.1% [51.7, 52.5]
	High risk	59.1% [58.3, 59.9]	63.7% [61.6, 65.7]	58.4% [57.6, 59.2]
1.5-mile run	Low risk	49.2% [49.1, 49.4]	51.6% [51.2, 51.9]	48.6% [48.4, 48.8]
	Moderate risk	49.8% [49.4, 50.2]	50.4% [49.5, 51.3]	49.6% [49.2, 50.1]
	High risk	52.6% [52.1, 53.2]	51.4% [48.1, 54.4]	52.7% [52.1, 53.2]
Push-ups	Low risk	49.2% [49.0, 49.4]	49.6% [49.0, 50.1]	49.2% [49.0, 49.4]
	Moderate risk	50.2% [49.9, 50.4]	53.5% [53.0, 54.1]	49.1% [48.8, 49.4]
	High risk	51.4% [50.9, 51.8]	52.1% [51.3, 52.8]	51.0% [50.5, 51.5]
Sit-ups	Low risk	49.7% [49.5, 49.9]	51.7% [51.2, 52.1]	49.2% [49.0, 49.4]
	Moderate risk	50.0% [49.7, 50.4]	52.1% [51.4, 52.9]	49.5% [49.1, 49.9]
	High risk	50.3% [49.9, 50.7]	52.2% [51.3, 53.1]	49.8% [49.4, 50.3]

NOTE: For the survival analyses, we adapted low-, moderate-, and high-risk fitness categories based on the AF-FA scoring system (AFI 36-2905, 2020) for each of the four AF-FA components. Fitness scores for AC and cardiorespiratory endurance (i.e., the 1.5-mile run) are determined by AF standards, which we used to generate cutoffs for approximately equivalent fitness categories for push-ups and sit-ups. For AC, standards vary by gender, and for the 1.5-mile run, standards vary by gender and age. Values shown are the estimated percentages of airmen with first-year fitness scores in each of the designated categories who would likely receive specified health and injury diagnoses within their first four YOS. Values in brackets show 95-percent confidence intervals for the estimated percentages.

We also found differences between estimated hazard ratios of different races. For example, being in the high-risk category for AC is associated with a three- to four-times higher risk of diabetes for all races except for Asian service members, who have only a two-times higher risk. On the other hand, Asian service members in the high-risk category for the 1.5-mile run have a higher associated risk of diabetes than other races do. The results shown in Tables B.8 and B.9 suggest that the relationship between fitness and health outcomes varies by gender and race, and a more in-depth exploration could inform fitness standards that are appropriate for all airmen.

Table B.8. Estimated Incidence of Adverse Health Outcomes, by Diagnosis Type, Fitness Category, and Race

AF-FA Component	AF-FA Fitness Category	Estimated Percentage of Diagnosis Within First Four Years of Service				
		All Airmen	Asian or Pacific Islander	Black	Hispanic	White
Diabetes						
Overall incidence	All	1.63% [1.60, 1.67]	1.97% [1.78, 2.15]	2.35% [2.23, 2.46]	1.59% [1.48, 1.70]	1.46% [1.42, 1.50]
AC	Low risk	1.08% [1.04, 1.11]	1.48% [1.31, 1.66]	1.52% [1.42, 1.63]	1.11% [1.01, 1.21]	0.93% [0.90, 0.97]
	Moderate risk	2.73% [2.63, 2.84]	4.21% [3.44, 4.97]	4.35% [3.99, 4.72]	2.95% [2.58, 3.33]	2.36% [2.24, 2.47]
	High risk	5.81% [5.47, 6.14]	7.65% [4.74, 10.5]	8.31% [7.23, 9.37]	6.40% [5.07, 7.71]	5.18% [4.81, 5.55]
1.5-mile run	Low risk	1.25% [1.22, 1.29]	1.48% [1.30, 1.67]	1.82% [1.71, 1.94]	1.28% [1.17, 1.39]	1.11% [1.07, 1.15]
	Moderate risk	2.11% [1.99, 2.22]	2.81% [2.21, 3.40]	2.70% [2.39, 3.02]	2.30% [1.89, 2.71]	1.88% [1.74, 2.01]
	High risk	2.50% [2.34, 2.66]	3.03% [2.23, 3.83]	3.14% [2.71, 3.57]	2.83% [2.21, 3.46]	2.27% [2.08, 2.45]
Push-ups	Low risk	1.44% [1.39, 1.48]	1.86% [1.63, 2.09]	2.08% [1.93, 2.22]	1.36% [1.23, 1.50]	1.27% [1.22, 1.32]
	Moderate risk	1.53% [1.46, 1.59]	1.74% [1.40, 2.07]	2.28% [2.08, 2.48]	1.65% [1.45, 1.85]	1.33% [1.25, 1.40]
	High risk	2.09% [1.97, 2.21]	2.84% [2.05, 3.63]	2.68% [2.33, 3.03]	2.16% [1.73, 2.59]	1.95% [1.80, 2.09]
Sit-ups	Low risk	1.28% [1.24, 1.32]	1.59% [1.39, 1.79]	1.91% [1.79, 2.03]	1.29% [1.17, 1.41]	1.10% [1.06, 1.15]
	Moderate risk	1.81% [1.72, 1.90]	1.98% [1.53, 2.43]	2.87% [2.57, 3.17]	1.84% [1.55, 2.12]	1.58% [1.48, 1.69]
	High risk	2.51% [2.38, 2.63]	3.61% [2.85, 4.36]	3.44% [3.00, 3.88]	2.66% [2.21, 3.11]	2.30% [2.16, 2.44]
Hypertension						
Overall incidence	All	7.36% [7.28, 7.43]	6.16% [5.84, 6.49]	11.0% [10.7, 11.2]	4.79% [4.60, 4.97]	7.10% [7.01, 7.18]
AC	Low risk	4.83% [4.76, 4.90]	4.61% [4.31, 4.92]	7.36% [7.14, 7.58]	3.33% [3.15, 3.50]	4.54% [4.45, 4.62]
	Moderate risk	13.4% [13.2, 13.6]	14.3% [13.0, 15.7]	21.1% [20.4, 21.8]	9.85% [9.20, 10.5]	12.5% [12.2, 12.7]
	High risk	23.9% [23.3, 24.5]	23.6% [18.8, 28.2]	34.9% [33.0, 36.8]	17.2% [15.1, 19.2]	22.6% [21.9, 23.3]
1.5-mile run	Low risk	5.65% [5.57, 5.72]	4.66% [4.34, 4.98]	8.46% [8.22, 8.71]	3.93% [3.74, 4.12]	5.46% [5.37, 5.55]
	Moderate risk	9.99% [9.75, 10.2]	8.66% [7.64, 9.67]	13.3% [12.6, 13.9]	7.50% [6.78, 8.21]	9.61% [9.32, 9.90]
	High risk	13.4% [13.0, 13.7]	11.7% [10.2, 13.2]	18.7% [17.7, 19.6]	9.34% [8.26, 10.4]	12.7% [12.2, 13.1]
Push-ups	Low risk	7.17% [7.07, 7.27]	6.21% [5.80, 6.61]	11.1% [10.8, 11.4]	4.79% [4.55, 5.04]	6.82% [6.70, 6.94]

Estimated Percentage of Diagnosis Within First Four Years of Service

AF-FA Component	AF-FA Fitness Category	All Airmen	Asian or Pacific Islander	Black	Hispanic	White
	Moderate risk	6.35% [6.22, 6.47]	4.87% [4.31, 5.42]	9.26% [8.86, 9.65]	4.13% [3.82, 4.45]	6.20% [6.05, 6.34]
	High risk	8.15% [7.92, 8.34]	7.21% [5.98, 8.43]	10.7% [10.0, 11.4]	5.27% [4.63, 5.91]	8.04% [7.77, 8.32]
Sit-ups	Low risk	5.96% [5.88, 6.04]	5.06% [4.71, 5.40]	9.60% [9.34, 9.86]	4.08% [3.87, 4.28]	5.51% [5.41, 5.61]
	Moderate risk	8.25% [8.06, 8.43]	7.33% [6.47, 8.17]	12.4% [11.8, 13.0]	5.01% [4.55, 5.46]	8.01% [7.79, 8.22]
	High risk	11.0% [10.8, 11.3]	9.59% [8.38, 10.8]	14.0% [13.2, 14.8]	8.13% [7.37, 8.88]	11.1% [10.8, 11.3]
Other cardiovascular disease						
Overall incidence	All	30.2% [30.1, 30.3]	24.4% [23.9, 25.0]	35.1% [34.7, 35.4]	27.2% [26.8, 27.6]	30.1% [29.9, 30.2]
AC	Low risk	27.6% [27.5, 27.8]	22.9% [22.3, 23.5]	32.0% [31.6, 32.4]	25.7% [25.2, 26.1]	27.4% [27.2, 27.6]
	Moderate risk	36.4% [36.0, 36.7]	31.5% [29.7, 33.2]	43.5% [42.6, 44.4]	32.3% [31.3, 33.3]	35.9% [35.5, 36.2]
	High risk	44.8% [44.0, 45.5]	43.2% [37.6, 48.4]	52.2% [50.2, 54.2]	39.9% [37.2, 42.5]	44.0% [43.1, 44.8]
1.5-mile run	Low risk	28.4% [28.3, 28.6]	23.3% [22.7, 24.0]	32.9% [32.4, 33.3]	26.1% [25.7, 26.5]	28.3% [28.2, 28.5]
	Moderate risk	32.1% [31.7, 32.5]	26.0% [24.4, 27.6]	36.7% [35.7, 37.6]	30.1% [28.8, 31.3]	31.7% [31.3, 32.2]
	High risk	34.7% [34.2, 35.2]	26.6% [24.6, 28.7]	38.5% [37.3, 39.8]	30.5% [28.8, 32.2]	34.8% [34.2, 35.4]
Push-ups	Low risk	29.1% [28.9, 29.3]	24.2% [23.5, 24.9]	33.8% [33.3, 34.2]	26.6% [26.1, 27.1]	29.0% [28.8, 29.2]
	Moderate risk	29.9% [29.6, 30.1]	23.9% [22.8, 25.0]	34.4% [33.7, 35.0]	26.9% [26.2, 27.6]	29.8% [29.5, 30.1]
	High risk	32.0% [31.6, 32.4]	24.1% [22.0, 26.1]	37.3% [36.2, 38.3]	28.9% [27.6, 30.2]	31.8% [31.3, 32.2]
Sit-ups	Low risk	28.8% [28.6, 28.9]	23.6% [22.9, 24.2]	33.5% [33.1, 34.0]	26.4% [25.9, 26.9]	28.5% [28.3, 28.7]
	Moderate risk	31.1% [30.8, 31.5]	26.1% [24.6, 27.5]	36.8% [35.9, 37.6]	27.8% [26.8, 28.7]	30.9% [30.6, 31.3]
	High risk	32.9% [32.5, 33.2]	24.9% [23.1, 26.7]	37.3% [36.1, 38.5]	29.1% [27.8, 30.3]	33.1% [32.6, 33.5]
Overuse injuries						
Overall incidence	All	58.0% [57.9, 58.2]	52.1% [51.4, 52.7]	62.4% [62.0, 62.8]	58.9% [58.4, 59.3]	57.3% [57.2, 57.5]
AC	Low risk	55.9% [55.7, 56.0]	50.5% [49.8, 51.3]	60.1% [59.6, 60.5]	57.5% [57.0, 58.0]	55.0% [54.8, 55.2]
	Moderate risk	63.0% [62.7, 63.3]	59.1% [57.1, 61.0]	68.4% [67.5, 69.3]	63.5% [62.4, 64.6]	62.2% [61.8, 62.6]
	High risk	71.1% [70.4, 71.8]	66.9% [61.0, 71.9]	76.2% [74.3, 78.0]	68.4% [65.5, 71.0]	70.5% [69.5, 71.3]
1.5-mile run	Low risk	56.6% [56.4, 56.7]	51.3% [50.6, 52.1]	61.3% [60.8, 61.7]	58.0% [57.5, 58.5]	55.7% [55.5, 55.9]
	Moderate risk	59.3% [58.9, 59.7]	51.7% [49.8, 53.6]	62.3% [61.2, 63.3]	60.5% [59.0, 61.9]	58.9% [58.3, 59.4]

Estimated Percentage of Diagnosis Within First Four Years of Service

AF-FA Component	AF-FA Fitness Category	All Airmen	Asian or Pacific Islander	Black	Hispanic	White
	High risk	61.0% [60.5, 61.5]	52.2% [49.8, 54.6]	62.0% [60.7, 63.3]	61.2% [59.2, 63.1]	61.3% [60.7, 61.9]
Push-ups	Low risk	56.5% [56.3, 56.7]	51.5% [50.7, 52.4]	61.5% [61.0, 62.0]	58.1% [57.5, 58.7]	55.5% [55.3, 55.7]
	Moderate risk	57.8% [57.6, 58.1]	51.6% [50.2, 52.9]	61.4% [60.7, 62.1]	58.4% [57.6, 59.2]	57.3% [57.0, 57.7]
	High risk	61.5% [61.1, 61.9]	52.0% [49.4, 54.4]	63.9% [62.7, 65.0]	61.2% [59.7, 62.6]	61.4% [60.9, 61.9]
Sit-ups	Low risk	56.7% [56.5, 56.9]	51.1% [50.3, 51.9]	61.7% [61.3, 62.2]	58.3% [57.8, 58.8]	55.7% [55.5, 55.9]
	Moderate risk	59.0% [58.6, 59.3]	53.6% [51.9, 55.2]	61.9% [60.9, 62.8]	59.1% [58.1, 60.2]	58.6% [58.2, 59.1]
	High risk	59.7% [59.3, 60.1]	51.9% [49.8, 54.0]	62.3% [61.0, 63.5]	59.3% [57.9, 60.8]	59.8% [59.3, 60.2]
Other musculoskeletal conditions						
Overall incidence	All	50.3% [50.1, 50.4]	46.2% [45.5, 46.9]	53.7% [53.3, 54.1]	52% [51.5, 52.4]	49.6% [49.4, 49.7]
AC	Low risk	48.9% [48.7, 49.0]	45.0% [44.2, 45.7]	52.4% [52.0, 52.8]	51.0% [50.5, 51.5]	48.1% [47.9, 48.3]
	Moderate risk	52.9% [52.6, 53.2]	51.4% [49.4, 53.4]	56.0% [55.1, 57.0]	54.6% [53.5, 55.8]	52.2% [51.8, 52.6]
	High risk	59.1% [58.3, 59.9]	59.6% [53.4, 65.0]	62.4% [60.3, 64.4]	61.4% [58.5, 64.0]	58.2% [57.3, 59.1]
1.5-mile run	Low risk	49.2% [49.1, 49.4]	45.5% [44.7, 46.3]	53.3% [52.9, 53.8]	51.4% [50.9, 51.8]	48.3% [48.1, 48.5]
	Moderate risk	49.8% [49.4, 50.2]	45.5% [43.6, 47.4]	50.2% [49.2, 51.3]	52.4% [50.9, 53.8]	49.7% [49.2, 50.2]
	High risk	52.6% [52.1, 53.2]	48.1% [45.7, 50.4]	53.7% [52.4, 55.0]	52.9% [50.9, 54.8]	52.6% [52.0, 53.3]
Push-ups	Low risk	49.2% [49.0, 49.4]	46.3% [45.4, 47.1]	54.1% [53.6, 54.6]	51.6% [51.0, 52.2]	48.1% [47.8, 48.3]
	Moderate risk	50.2% [49.9, 50.4]	45.0% [43.7, 46.3]	52.7% [52.0, 53.4]	51.2% [50.4, 52.0]	49.8% [49.5, 50.1]
	High risk	51.4% [50.9, 51.8]	44.7% [42.2, 47.1]	50.4% [49.2, 51.5]	52.6% [51.1, 54.1]	51.7% [51.2, 52.2]
Sit-ups	Low risk	49.7% [49.5, 49.9]	45.7% [44.8, 46.5]	54.0% [53.5, 54.4]	51.7% [51.2, 52.3]	48.7% [48.5, 48.9]
	Moderate risk	50.0% [49.7, 50.4]	46.5% [44.8, 48.1]	51.7% [50.8, 52.7]	51.4% [50.3, 52.4]	49.7% [49.2, 50.1]
	High risk	50.3% [49.9, 50.7]	46.3% [44.2, 48.4]	50.3% [49.0, 51.5]	51.4% [49.9, 52.8]	50.4% [49.9, 50.8]

NOTE: For the survival analyses, we adapted low-, moderate-, and high-risk fitness categories based on the AF-FA scoring system (AFI 36-2905, 2020) for each of the four AF-FA components. Fitness scores for AC and cardiorespiratory endurance (i.e., the 1.5-mile run) are determined by AF standards, which we used to generate cutoffs for approximately equivalent fitness categories for push-ups and sit-ups. For AC, standards vary by gender, and for the 1.5-mile run, standards vary by gender and age. Values shown are the estimated percentages of airmen with first-year FA scores in each of the designated fitness categories who would be likely to receive the specified diagnosis within their first four YOS. Values in parenthesis show the 95-percent confidence intervals for the estimated percentages.

Table B.9. Estimated Hazard Ratios of Adverse Health Outcomes, by Diagnosis Type, Fitness Category, and Race

AF-FA Component	AF-FA Fitness Category	All Airmen	Asian or Pacific Islander	Black	Hispanic	Other	Unknown	White
Diabetes								
AC	Moderate risk	1.86 [1.80, 1.91]	2.06 [1.81, 2.33]	1.99 [1.86, 2.13]	1.78 [1.62, 1.96]	1.90 [1.48, 2.43]	2.01 [1.46, 2.78]	1.82 [1.75, 1.89]
	High risk	3.53 [3.35, 3.73]	1.97 [1.37, 2.83]	4.11 [3.66, 4.62]	3.60 [3.00, 4.32]	4.39 [2.93, 6.59]	4.73 [2.62, 8.54]	3.42 [3.20, 3.66]
1.5-mile run	Moderate risk	1.40 [1.35, 1.44]	1.36 [1.18, 1.56]	1.32 [1.23, 1.42]	1.46 [1.31, 1.62]	1.28 [0.97, 1.70]	1.20 [0.83, 1.74]	1.42 [1.36, 1.48]
	High risk	1.94 [1.85, 2.04]	2.15 [1.75, 2.64]	1.73 [1.56, 1.92]	1.93 [1.62, 2.29]	2.81 [1.95, 4.06]	1.59 [0.89, 2.84]	1.98 [1.86, 2.11]
Push-ups	Moderate risk	1.04 [1.00, 1.08]	1.00 [0.84, 1.19]	1.09 [1.00, 1.19]	1.08 [0.96, 1.22]	0.77 [0.57, 1.04]	1.05 [0.70, 1.56]	1.02 [0.97, 1.07]
	High risk	1.02 [0.96, 1.08]	1.07 [0.81, 1.41]	1.04 [0.91, 1.18]	0.85 [0.70, 1.04]	0.42 [0.24, 0.73]	1.07 [0.59, 1.96]	1.06 [0.98, 1.14]
Sit-ups	Moderate risk	1.20 [1.15, 1.24]	1.07 [0.90, 1.28]	1.31 [1.20, 1.43]	1.16 [1.02, 1.30]	1.27 [0.94, 1.70]	0.88 [0.56, 1.37]	1.18 [1.13, 1.24]
	High risk	1.38 [1.31, 1.45]	1.72 [1.38, 2.14]	1.36 [1.18, 1.55]	1.22 [1.03, 1.45]	1.61 [1.10, 2.37]	0.94 [0.52, 1.69]	1.38 [1.30, 1.47]
Hypertension								
AC	Moderate risk	2.01 [1.97, 2.04]	2.06 [1.88, 2.25]	1.95 [1.87, 2.03]	2.09 [1.96, 2.23]	1.97 [1.68, 2.32]	2.09 [1.72, 2.54]	2.02 [1.98, 2.07]
	High risk	3.25 [3.16, 3.35]	3.13 [2.56, 3.83]	2.99 [2.79, 3.21]	3.64 [3.24, 4.09]	2.92 [2.21, 3.87]	3.85 [2.76, 5.38]	3.31 [3.19, 3.44]
1.5-mile run	Moderate risk	1.35 [1.32, 1.38]	1.38 [1.25, 1.52]	1.26 [1.21, 1.31]	1.39 [1.29, 1.49]	1.42 [1.19, 1.70]	1.27 [1.02, 1.60]	1.37 [1.34, 1.41]
	High risk	1.85 [1.81, 1.90]	1.92 [1.69, 2.18]	1.70 [1.61, 1.79]	1.96 [1.77, 2.16]	2.39 [1.90, 2.99]	1.84 [1.36, 2.49]	1.89 [1.83, 1.95]
Push-ups	Moderate risk	0.98 [0.96, 1.01]	1.07 [0.95, 1.20]	1.01 [0.96, 1.06]	0.96 [0.88, 1.04]	0.87 [0.72, 1.06]	0.94 [0.73, 1.19]	0.98 [0.95, 1.00]
	High risk	1.00 [0.97, 1.03]	1.12 [0.92, 1.36]	1.06 [0.98, 1.14]	1.04 [0.91, 1.18]	0.82 [0.60, 1.12]	0.73 [0.50, 1.07]	0.98 [0.94, 1.02]
Sit-ups	Moderate risk	1.16 [1.13, 1.18]	1.09 [0.97, 1.22]	1.16 [1.10, 1.22]	1.24 [1.15, 1.34]	1.17 [0.97, 1.43]	0.98 [0.75, 1.28]	1.15 [1.12, 1.19]
	High risk	1.30 [1.27, 1.34]	1.21 [1.04, 1.42]	1.26 [1.17, 1.36]	1.26 [1.13, 1.40]	1.24 [0.97, 1.59]	1.34 [0.99, 1.81]	1.32 [1.27, 1.36]
Other cardiovascular disease								
AC	Moderate risk	1.34 [1.32, 1.35]	1.39 [1.31, 1.46]	1.38 [1.34, 1.41]	1.33 [1.29, 1.38]	1.22 [1.12, 1.33]	1.42 [1.27, 1.57]	1.32 [1.31, 1.34]
	High risk	1.74 [1.71, 1.78]	2.18 [1.90, 2.51]	1.81 [1.72, 1.91]	1.70 [1.58, 1.83]	1.57 [1.31, 1.88]	1.47 [1.16, 1.88]	1.73 [1.68, 1.77]
1.5-mile run	Moderate risk	1.12 [1.11, 1.13]	1.13 [1.07, 1.19]	1.09 [1.07, 1.12]	1.13 [1.09, 1.17]	1.27 [1.16, 1.40]	1.13 [1.01, 1.28]	1.12 [1.11, 1.14]
	High risk	1.42 [1.40, 1.44]	1.35 [1.25, 1.46]	1.39 [1.34, 1.44]	1.54 [1.46, 1.62]	1.57 [1.37, 1.80]	1.57 [1.33, 1.86]	1.42 [1.39, 1.44]
Push-ups	Moderate risk	1.03 [1.02, 1.04]	1.07 [1.02, 1.14]	1.05 [1.02, 1.08]	1.01 [0.98, 1.05]	0.95 [0.87, 1.05]	1.06 [0.94, 1.19]	1.02 [1.01, 1.03]

The column group "Estimated Hazard Ratio for Diagnosis (Relative to the Low-Risk Category)" spans the race columns.

Estimated Hazard Ratio for Diagnosis (Relative to the Low-Risk Category)

AF-FA Component	AF-FA Fitness Category	All Airmen	Asian or Pacific Islander	Black	Hispanic	Other	Unknown	White
	High risk	1.05 [1.03, 1.06]	1.14 [1.03, 1.25]	1.05 [1.01, 1.10]	1.05 [1.00, 1.11]	0.92 [0.79, 1.06]	1.07 [0.90, 1.27]	1.04 [1.02, 1.06]
Sit-ups	Moderate risk	1.05 [1.04, 1.06]	1.09 [1.03, 1.16]	1.02 [0.99, 1.05]	1.04 [1.00, 1.08]	1.17 [1.06, 1.30]	0.96 [0.84, 1.10]	1.05 [1.04, 1.07]
	High risk	1.08 [1.07, 1.10]	1.11 [1.02, 1.21]	1.09 [1.04, 1.14]	1.02 [0.97, 1.08]	1.20 [1.05, 1.37]	1.19 [1.01, 1.39]	1.09 [1.07, 1.11]
Other musculoskeletal conditions								
AC	Moderate risk	1.22 [1.21, 1.23]	1.32 [1.26, 1.39]	1.23 [1.20, 1.26]	1.22 [1.18, 1.25]	1.12 [1.04, 1.21]	1.10 [0.99, 1.21]	1.21 [1.20, 1.22]
	High risk	1.49 [1.46, 1.52]	1.66 [1.44, 1.90]	1.49 [1.41, 1.57]	1.55 [1.45, 1.65]	1.47 [1.25, 1.73]	1.61 [1.31, 1.97]	1.48 [1.44, 1.51]
1.5-mile run	Moderate risk	1.01 [1.00, 1.02]	1.01 [0.96, 1.05]	0.97 [0.95, 0.99]	1.01 [0.98, 1.04]	1.07 [0.99, 1.17]	1.01 [0.91, 1.13]	1.02 [1.00, 1.03]
	High risk	1.20 [1.18, 1.22]	1.10 [1.03, 1.17]	1.10 [1.06, 1.14]	1.23 [1.18, 1.29]	1.13 [0.99, 1.28]	1.28 [1.11, 1.49]	1.23 [1.21, 1.25]
Push-ups	Moderate risk	1.00 [0.99, 1.01]	0.99 [0.95, 1.04]	1.02 [1.00, 1.04]	1.00 [0.98, 1.03]	0.95 [0.88, 1.03]	1.04 [0.94, 1.14]	0.99 [0.98, 1.00]
	High risk	1.03 [1.02, 1.04]	1.02 [0.94, 1.11]	1.00 [0.96, 1.03]	1.05 [1.00, 1.10]	1.02 [0.91, 1.14]	1.01 [0.87, 1.17]	1.03 [1.01, 1.05]
Sit-ups	Moderate risk	0.97 [0.96, 0.97]	0.97 [0.92, 1.02]	0.96 [0.93, 0.98]	0.97 [0.94, 1.00]	0.93 [0.85, 1.02]	0.99 [0.89, 1.11]	0.97 [0.95, 0.98]
	High risk	0.97 [0.96, 0.99]	0.93 [0.87, 1.00]	0.91 [0.87, 0.94]	0.94 [0.90, 0.98]	1.04 [0.93, 1.16]	0.84 [0.73, 0.97]	0.99 [0.97, 1.00]
Overuse injuries								
AC	Moderate risk	1.19 [1.18, 1.19]	1.23 [1.17, 1.29]	1.22 [1.20, 1.25]	1.18 [1.15, 1.21]	1.11 [1.03, 1.19]	1.17 [1.07, 1.27]	1.18 [1.16, 1.19]
	High risk	1.48 [1.45, 1.51]	1.59 [1.40, 1.81]	1.52 [1.45, 1.60]	1.46 [1.37, 1.56]	1.33 [1.13, 1.56]	1.73 [1.44, 2.08]	1.47 [1.43, 1.50]
1.5-mile run	Moderate risk	1.04 [1.03, 1.05]	1.01 [0.96, 1.05]	1.02 [1.00, 1.04]	1.04 [1.01, 1.07]	1.10 [1.01, 1.19]	1.14 [1.04, 1.25]	1.05 [1.04, 1.06]
	High risk	1.25 [1.24, 1.27]	1.13 [1.06, 1.20]	1.16 [1.13, 1.20]	1.27 [1.22, 1.33]	1.25 [1.12, 1.41]	1.20 [1.04, 1.39]	1.29 [1.27, 1.31]
Push-ups	Moderate risk	1.03 [1.02, 1.03]	1.02 [0.97, 1.06]	1.03 [1.01, 1.05]	1.01 [0.98, 1.03]	1.04 [0.97, 1.12]	0.99 [0.90, 1.08]	1.03 [1.02, 1.04]
	High risk	1.08 [1.06, 1.09]	1.04 [0.97, 1.12]	1.04 [1.01, 1.08]	1.11 [1.06, 1.15]	1.05 [0.94, 1.17]	1.05 [0.92, 1.20]	1.08 [1.07, 1.10]
Sit-ups	Moderate risk	0.99 [0.98, 1.00]	0.98 [0.94, 1.03]	1.00 [0.98, 1.03]	0.98 [0.95, 1.00]	0.99 [0.91, 1.07]	0.97 [0.88, 1.07]	0.99 [0.98, 1.00]
	High risk	1.00 [0.99, 1.01]	0.98 [0.92, 1.04]	0.96 [0.93, 1.00]	0.98 [0.94, 1.02]	1.07 [0.96, 1.18]	0.85 [0.75, 0.97]	1.01 [1.00, 1.02]

NOTE: For each of the four fitness components, we adapted low-, moderate-, or high-risk fitness categories based on the AF fitness scoring system (AFI 36-2905, 2020). Values shown are the estimated hazard ratios (e.g., 1.86 times greater risk) for airmen of receiving diagnoses over the course of their careers if their fitness falls into the moderate- or high-risk categories (relative to airmen with fitness in the low-risk category). Hazard ratios are estimated controlling for all fitness categories and individual demographics. Values in parenthesis show the 95-percent confidence intervals for the estimated hazard ratios.

Finally, Table B.10 shows the fitness categories cutoff values.

Table B.10. Fitness Category Cutoff Values

AF-FA Component (Measure)	Fitness Category	Age Group	Female Airmen	Male Airmen
AC (inches)	Low risk	All	<= 31.5	<= 35
	Moderate risk	All	<= 35	<= 39
	High risk	All	> 35	> 39
1.5-mile run (seconds)	Low risk	< 30	<= 892	<= 753
	Moderate risk	< 30	<= 982	<= 816
	High risk	< 30	> 982	> 816
1.5-mile run (seconds)	Low risk	30–39	<= 920	<= 773
	Moderate risk	30–39	<= 1,017	<= 840
	High risk	30–39	> 1,017	> 840
1.5-mile run (seconds)	Low risk	40–49	<= 982	<= 816
	Moderate risk	40–49	<= 1,094	<= 892
	High risk	40–49	> 1,094	> 892
1.5-mile run (seconds)	Low risk	50–59	<= 1,094	<= 892
	Moderate risk	50–59	<= 1,183	<= 982
	High risk	50–59	> 1,183	> 982
1.5-mile run (seconds)	Low risk	60 and older	<= 1,183	<= 982
	Moderate risk	60 and older	<= 1,348	<= 1,094
	High risk	60 and older	> 1,348	> 1,094
Push-ups (repetitions/minute)	Low risk	< 30	>= 34	>= 51
	Moderate risk	< 30	>= 24	>= 39
	High risk	< 30	< 24	< 39
Push-ups (repetitions/minute)	Low risk	30–39	>= 32	>= 42
	Moderate risk	30–39	>= 21	>= 31
	High risk	30–39	< 21	< 31
Push-ups (repetitions/minute)	Low risk	40–49	>= 27	>= 32
	Moderate risk	40–49	>= 17	>= 23
	High risk	40–49	< 17	< 23
Push-ups (repetitions/minute)	Low risk	50–59	>= 23	>= 32
	Moderate risk	50–59	>= 15	>= 22
	High risk	50–59	< 15	< 22

AF-FA Component (Measure)	Fitness Category	Age Group	Female Airmen	Male Airmen
Push-ups (repetitions/minute)	Low risk	60 and older	>= 14	>= 22
	Moderate risk	60 and older	>= 9	>= 15
	High risk	60 and older	< 9	< 15
Sit-ups (repetitions/minute)	Low risk	< 30	>= 44	>= 49
	Moderate risk	< 30	>= 36	>= 42
	High risk	< 30	< 36	< 42
Sit-ups (repetitions/minute)	Low risk	30–39	>= 35	>= 45
	Moderate risk	30–39	>= 27	>= 37
	High risk	30–39	< 27	< 37
Sit-ups (repetitions/minute)	Low risk	40–49	>= 31	>= 41
	Moderate risk	40–49	>= 22	>= 33
	High risk	40–49	< 22	< 33
Sit-ups (repetitions/minute)	Low risk	50–59	>= 23	>= 36
	Moderate risk	50–59	>= 16	>= 28
	High risk	50–59	< 16	< 28
Sit-ups (repetitions/minute)	Low risk	60 and older	>= 21	>= 32
	Moderate risk	60 and older	>= 12	>= 23
	High risk	60 and older	< 12	< 23

NOTE: For each of the four fitness components, we adapted low-, moderate-, or high-risk fitness categories based on the AF fitness scoring system (AFI 36-2905, 2020). The AFI provides cutoffs for these fitness categories for the AC and 1.5-mile run components, and we developed cutoffs for push-ups and sit-ups using the same relative quantiles.

Appendix C. Interview Protocol

A. Background

[I would like to start by asking you a few questions regarding your background.]

A1. Which component are you in: Active, Reserve, or Guard?

A2. What is your current rank or grade?

A3. What is your career field?

A4. How many years of service have you provided since [commissioning/enlisting] in the Air Force?

A5. How many months or years do you have remaining on your current service obligation?

[We would now like to ask you about fitness in the Air Force. We recognize that COVID-19, also known as the coronavirus, has likely had a substantial impact on Air Force fitness. However, for these questions, we would like you to focus on and respond regarding your experiences before the COVID-19 pandemic began affecting local community and Air Force operations (that is, before March 2020). In other words, please respond regarding what happened when standard Air Force operations were in place.]

B. Culture of Fitness

[For the next set of questions, I would like to ask you about the Air Force culture of fitness.]

B1.1. What messages, if any, [have you/has your squadron leadership] communicated to your unit regarding maintaining physical fitness?

- *Probes (ask as needed):*
    - *How [have you/has your squadron leadership] communicated [this message/these messages]?*
    - *How often [do you/does your squadron leadership] communicate [this message/these messages]?*
    - *How, if at all, have the messages communicated by [you/squadron leadership] affected your unit's level of physical activity?*

B1.2. What actions, if any, [have you/has your squadron leadership] taken to promote physical fitness in your unit?

- *Probes:*
  - *What, if any, [squadron-, group-, wing-] level activities [have you/has your squadron leadership] implemented to promote physical fitness in your unit?*
  - *How, if at all, [have you/has your squadron leadership] worked to ensure that people in your unit have time to maintain physical fitness?*
  - *What resources, if any, [do you/does your squadron leadership] make available for maintaining physical fitness? Resources can include equipment, funding for fitness activities, and so forth.*
- B1.2A. How, if at all, have the actions taken by [you/your squadron leadership] to promote physical fitness affected your unit's level of physical activity?

B1.3. How, if at all, [do you/does your squadron leadership] reward those who maintain physical fitness?

B1.4. How, if at all, [do you/does your squadron leadership] enforce any consequences for those who do not meet minimum standards for physical fitness?

B1.5. What could [you/your squadron leadership] do to make it easier for you or other airmen in your unit to stay physically fit?

B1.6. What else, if anything, should [you/your squadron leadership] do to better promote physical fitness in your unit?

B1.7. Are you aware of any promising programs that other units have implemented to promote physical fitness? If so, please describe.
- B1.7A. What about the program(s) is/are promising?

B1.8. How, if at all, has COVID-19 impacted the culture of fitness in the Air Force?

C. Barriers to Fitness

[*I'd like to move to a few questions that address barriers to physical fitness.*]

C1. Broadly, what factors do you think contribute to airmen *not* getting enough exercise?

C2. More specifically, what aspects of work in your unit do airmen find to be most challenging as far as staying physically fit?
- *Probes:*

> - *What things about your work tasks make it difficult for you to stay physically fit?*
> - *What things about the way work is organized make it difficult for you to stay physically fit?*
> - *What aspects of your work prevent you from engaging in physical fitness outside of work?*

C3. What, if any, aspects of your unit make it challenging to stay physically fit?

C4. What, if any, aspects of your installation make it challenging to stay physically fit?

C5. What could the Air Force do to make it easier for airmen to stay physically fit?

C6. How, if at all, has COVID-19 impacted barriers to fitness in the Air Force?

D. Fitness Information

[As part of this project, we would like to better understand what airmen know about the Tier 1 Air Force fitness assessment, which includes four components: a 1.5-mile run or 1.0-mile walk, abdominal circumference (AC) measurement, push-ups, and sit-ups. *If asked, we are not addressing the operationally relevant Tier 2 tests.*]

D1. Air Force Fitness Assessment Knowledge

D1.1. In general, what do airmen know regarding the Air Force fitness assessment?

- *Probes:*
    - *What do they know about the components of the fitness assessment?*
    - *What do they know about the [scientific] rationale for the components of the fitness assessment?*
    - *What do they know about the frequency of the fitness assessment?*
    - *What do they know about going on profile?[44]*

D1.2. What is your current impression of the Air Force fitness assessment?

- D1.2A. Why do you have this impression of the fitness assessment?

D1.3. What additional information would you like to have about the Air Force fitness assessment?

---

[44] Going *on profile* refers to receiving a medical exemption or waiver.

D1.4. How, if at all, has the information communicated to you about the Air Force fitness assessment influenced your physical fitness activities?

D2. Air Force Fitness Assessment Preparation

D2.1. What actions do airmen in your unit take to prepare for the Air Force fitness assessment?

D2.2. About how much time before the fitness assessment do airmen in your unit begin to prepare for the fitness assessment [*days, weeks, months*]?

- D2.2A. Why do airmen take this amount of time?

D2.3. How does your immediate leadership respond to those who have received a medical waiver, or are "on profile," for the fitness assessment?

- *Probes:*

  - *Does your immediate leadership encourage or discourage people to go on profile? Explain.*
  - *When people are on profile, how does your immediate leadership behave toward them?*
  - *Have people in your unit gone on profile when they probably didn't need to? If so, please describe.*

D2.4. What, if any, negative behaviors are you aware of airmen engaging in to prepare for the Air Force fitness assessment?

- *Probe: Have airmen engaged in extreme dieting? Used diet pills or laxatives? Over-exercised?*

D2.5. How, if at all, has COVID-19 changed how airmen prepare for the Air Force fitness assessment?

E. Current Fitness Assessment

[I'd now like to ask a few questions regarding perceptions of and experiences with the current Air Force fitness assessment.]

E1. How do airmen perceive the components of the current Air Force fitness assessment?

- *Probes:*

  - *What do they think about the inclusion of each component?*
  - *What do they think about the minimum requirements of each component?*

– *What do they think about how testers evaluate airmen on each component?*

E2. Should the Air Force replace any of the Air Force fitness test components or keep the test as it currently is? Why or why not?

E3. Is the current fitness assessment fair or not fair to all airmen? Please explain.

- *Probe: Is it fairly administered to all airmen?*

E4. What actions can the Air Force take to prevent airmen from taking negative actions to prepare for the Air Force fitness assessment?

E5. How can the Air Force better use the Air Force fitness assessment to encourage airmen to stay physically fit throughout the year?

E6. What, if anything, should the Air Force do when it resumes administering the Air Force fitness assessment [*that is, when COVID-19 restrictions have been lifted*]?

F. Readiness

[I'd now like to ask a few questions regarding readiness.]

F1. Job Readiness

F1.1. Do you feel the current Air Force fitness assessment is an accurate or inaccurate measurement of readiness to perform the job requirements of your AFSC, or career field? Please explain.

- *Probe: If you did not do well on the Air Force fitness assessment, how, if at all, would your job be affected?*

F1.2. Does the current Air Force fitness assessment encourage or discourage airmen to maintain readiness to perform the job requirements of their AFSC, or career field? Please explain.

F1.3. How, if at all, could policies and practices regarding the current Air Force fitness assessment be changed to better support job readiness?

F2. Deployment Readiness

F2.1. Do you feel the current Air Force fitness assessment is an accurate or inaccurate measurement of readiness to deploy? Please explain.

- *Probe: If you did not do well on the Air Force fitness assessment, how, if at all, would your readiness to deploy be affected?*

F2.2. Does the current Air Force fitness assessment support an airman's readiness to do their deployed job? Please explain.

- *Probe: Does it help maintain readiness to do the physical components of their deployed job? Please explain.*

F2.3. How, if at all, could policies and practices regarding the current Air Force fitness assessment be changed to better support deployment readiness?

F2.4. How can the Air Force ensure fitness for deployment in times of COVID-19?

References

AFI—*See* Air Force Instruction.

Air Force Guidance Memorandum 2018-36-02, "ALO and TACP Tier 2 Operator Fitness Test Guidance Memorandum," Washington, D.C.: Department of the Air Force, June 1, 2018.

Air Force Instruction 36-2905, *Air Force Physical Fitness Program*, Washington, D.C.: Department of the Air Force, December 11, 2020.

Air Force Instruction 36-2501, *Officer Promotions and Selective Continuation*, Washington, D.C.: Department of the Air Force, July 16, 2004.

Air Force Manual 36-2905, *Air Force Physical Fitness Program*, Washington, D.C.: Department of the Air Force, December 11, 2020.

Asch, Beth J., John A. Romley, and Mark E. Totten, *The Quality of Personnel in the Enlisted Ranks*, Santa Monica, Calif.: RAND Corporation, MG-324-OSD, 2005. As of March 8, 2022:
https://www.rand.org/pubs/monographs/MG324.html

Ashwell, Margaret, and Sigrid Gibson, "Waist-to-Height Ratio as an Indicator of 'Early Health Risk': Simpler and More Predictive Than Using a 'Matrix' Based on BMI and Waist Circumference," *BMJ Open*, Vol. 6, No. 3, March 14, 2016, pp. 1–7.

Blair, Steven N., Harold W. Kohl III, Ralph S. Paffenbarger, Debra G. Clark, Kenneth H. Cooper, and Larry W. Gibbons, "Physical Fitness and All-Cause Mortality: A Prospective Study of Healthy Men and Women," *JAMA*, Vol. 262, No. 17, 1989, pp. 2395–2401.

Cartwright, Donna J., "ICD-9-CM to ICD-10-CM Codes: What? Why? How?" *Advances in Wound Care*, Vol. 2, No. 10, November 2013, pp. 588–592.

CDC—*See* Centers for Disease Control and Prevention.

Centers for Disease Control and Prevention, "Defining Adult Overweight & Obesity," webpage, April 28, 2021. As of January 18, 2021:
https://www.cdc.gov/obesity/adult/defining.html

Chang, Yu-Kai, Jeffrey D. Labban, Jennifer I. Gapin, and Jennifer L. Etnier, "The Effects of Acute Exercise on Cognitive Performance: A Meta-Analysis," *Brain Research*, Vol. 1453, May 2012, pp. 87–101.

Cranston, Marcus M., Mark W. True, Jana L. Wardian, Rishawn M. Carriere, and Tom J. Sauerwein, "When Military Fitness Standards No Longer Apply: The High Prevalence of Metabolic Syndrome in Recent Air Force Retirees," *Military Medicine*, Vol. 182, No. 7, July 2017, pp. e1780–e1786.

Defense Health Agency, *DoD Health of the Force 2019*, Falls Church, Va., 2019.

Ervin, R. Bethene, "Prevalence of Metabolic Syndrome Among Adults 20 Years of Age and over, by Sex, Age, Race and Ethnicity, and Body Mass Index: United States, 2003–2006," *National Health Statistics Reports*, No. 13, May 2009, pp. 1–7.

Forcier, Kathleen, Laura R. Stroud, George D. Papandonatos, Brian Hitsman, Meredith Reiches, Jenelle Krishnamoorthy, and Raymond Niaura, "Links Between Physical Fitness and Cardiovascular Reactivity and Recovery to Psychological Stressors: A Meta-Analysis," *Health Psychology*, Vol. 25, No. 6, November 2006, pp. 723–739.

Hauret, Keith G., Bruce H. Jones, Steven H. Bullock, Michelle Canham-Chervak, and Sara Canada, "Musculoskeletal Injuries Description of an Under-Recognized Injury Problem Among Military Personnel," *American Journal of Preventative Medicine*, Vol. 38, No. 1 Suppl, January 2010, pp. S61–S70.

Hauschild, Veronique, David DeGroot, Shane Hall, Karen Deaver, Keith Hauret, Tyson Grier, and Bruce Jones, *Correlations Between Physical Fitness Tests and Performance of Military Tasks: A Systematic Review and Meta-Analyses*, Aberdeen Proving Ground, Md.: U.S. Army Public Health Command, Injury Prevention Program, ADA607688, June 2014.

Hauschild, Veronique, Keith Hauret, Melissa Richardson, Bruce H. Jones, and Terrence Lee, "A Taxonomy of Injuries for Public Health Monitoring and Reporting," Aberdeen Proving Ground, Md.: U.S. Army Public Health Command, Injury Prevention Program, Public Health Information Paper (PHIP) No. 12-01-0717, July 2017.

Hoffman, Jay R., David D. Church, and Mattan M. Hoffman, "Overuse Injuries in Military Personnel," in Amit Gefen and Yoram Epstein, eds., *The Mechanobiology and Mechanophysiology of Military-Related Injuries*, Vol. 19, Studies in Mechanobiology, Tissue Engineering and Biomaterials, Berlin: Springer International Publishing, 2016, pp. 141–161.

Honaker, James, Gary King, and Matthew Blackwell, "Amelia II: A Program for Missing Data," *Journal of Statistical Software*, Vol. 45, No. 7, 2011, pp. 1–47.

Kusnoor, Sheila V., Mallory N. Blasingame, Annette M. Williams, Spencer J. DesAutels, Jing Su, and Nunzia Bettinsoli Giuse, "A Narrative Review of the Impact of the Transition to ICD-10 and ICD-10-CM/PCS," *JAMIA Open*, Vol. 3, No. 1, April 2020, pp. 126–131.

Lim, Nelson, Louis T. Mariano, Amy G. Cox, David Schulker, and Lawrence M. Hanser, *Improving Demographic Diversity in the U.S. Air Force Officer Corps*, Santa Monica, Calif.: RAND Corporation, RR-495-AF, 2014. As of May 24, 2021: https://www.rand.org/pubs/research_reports/RR495.html

Mainor, Alexander J., Nancy E. Morden, Jeremy Smith, Stephanie Tomlin, and Jonathan Skinner, "ICD-10 Coding Will Challenge Researchers: Caution and Collaboration May Reduce Measurement Error and Improve Comparability over Time," *Medical Care*, Vol. 57, No. 7, July 2019, pp. e42–e46.

Marteau, Theresa M., "Screening for Cardiovascular Risk: Public Health Imperative or Matter for Individual Informed Choice?" *BMJ*, Vol. 325, No. 7355, July 2002, pp. 78–80.

Marteau, Theresa M., and Caryn Lerman, "Genetic Risk and Behavioural Change," *BMJ*, Vol. 322, No. 7293, April 2001, pp. 1056–1059.

Meadows, Sarah O., Charles C. Engel, Rebecca L. Collins, Robin Beckman, Matthew Cefalu, Jennifer Hawes-Dawson, Molly Doyle, Amii M. Kress, Lisa Sontag-Padilla, Rajeev Ramchand, and Kayla M. Williams, *2015 Department of Defense Health Related Behaviors Survey (HRBS)*, Santa Monica, Calif.: RAND Corporation, RR-1695-OSD, 2018. As of May 5, 2020: https://www.rand.org/pubs/research_reports/RR1695.html

Military Leadership Diversity Commission, *From Representation to Inclusion: Diversity Leadership for the 21st-Century Military*, Arlington, Va., March 2011.

National Research Council, *Assessing Fitness for Military Enlistment: Physical, Medical, and Mental Health Standards*, Washington, D.C.: National Academies Press, 2006.

Nye, Nathaniel S., Mary T. Pawlak, Bryant J. Webber, Juste N. Tchandja, and Michelle R. Milner, "Description and Rate of Musculoskeletal Injuries in Air Force Basic Military Trainees, 2012−2014," *Journal of Athletic Training*, Vol. 51, No. 11, 2016, pp. 858–865.

Palmer, Barbara, Michael E. Rench, Jon W. Carroll, and Stefan H. Constable, *Health and Job-Specific Body Composition Standards for the US Air Force*, Vol. 1: *Final Report*, Wright-Patterson Air Force Base, Ohio: Crew System Ergonomics Information Analysis Center, 2000.

Pearson, Emma, Harry Prapavessis, Christopher Higgins, Robert Petrella, Lauren White, and Marc Mitchell, "Adding Team-Based Financial Incentives to the Carrot Rewards Physical Activity App Increases Daily Step Count on a Population Scale: A 24-Week Matched Case Control Study," *International Journal of Behavioral Nutrition and Physical Activity*, Vol. 17, November 2020.

Pedersen, Cathrine, Hallgeir Halvari, and Anja H. Olafsen, "Worksite Physical Activity Intervention and Somatic Symptoms Burden: The Role of Coworker Support for Basic Psychological Needs and Autonomous Motivation," *Journal of Occupational Health Psychology*, Vol. 24, No. 1, February 2019, pp. 55–65.

Pronk, Nicolaas P., Brian Martinson, Ronald C. Kessler, Arne L. Beck, Gregory E. Simon, and Philip Wang, "The Association Between Work Performance and Physical Activity, Cardiorespiratory Fitness, and Obesity," *Journal of Occupational and Environmental Medicine*, Vol. 46, No. 1, January 2004, pp. 19–25.

Punthakee, Zubin, Ronald Goldenberg, and Pamela Katz, "Definition, Classification and Diagnosis of Diabetes, Prediabetes and Metabolic Syndrome," *Canadian Journal of Diabetes*, Vol. 42, April 2018, pp. S10–S15.

R Core Team, "R: A Language and Environment for Statistical Computing," R Foundation for Statistical Computing, Vienna, Austria, 2019. As of May 24, 2021:
https://www.R-project.org/

Reiner, Miriam, Christina Niermann, Darko Jekauc, and Alexander Woll, "Long-Term Health Benefits of Physical Activity—A Systematic Review of Longitudinal Studies," *BMC Public Health*, Vol. 13, September 2013.

Robbins, Anthony S., Susan Y. Chao, Christine R. Russ, and Vincent P. Fonseca, "Costs of Excess Body Weight Among Active Duty Personnel, U.S. Air Force, 1997," *Military Medicine*, Vol. 167, No. 5, May 2002, pp. 393–397.

Robson, Sean, Isabel Leamon, Maria C. Lytell, Miriam Matthews, and Margaret Chamberlin, *A Review of the Air Force Fitness Assessment*, Santa Monica, Calif.: RAND Corporation, RR-A762-1, 2021. As of September 21, 2021:
https://www.rand.org/pubs/research_reports/RRA762-1.html

Robson, Sean, Maria C. Lytell, Anthony Atler, Jason H. Campbell, and Carra S. Sims, *Physical Task Simulations: Performance Measures for the Validation of Physical Tests and Standards for Battlefield Airmen*, Santa Monica, Calif.: RAND Corporation, RR-1595-AF, 2020. As of September 21, 2021:
https://www.rand.org/pubs/research_reports/RR1595.html

Robson, Sean, Maria C. Lytell, Carra S. Sims, Stephanie Pezard, Thomas Manacapilli, Amanda Anderson, Therese Bohusch, and Abigail Haddad, *Fit for Duty? Evaluating the Physical Fitness Requirements of Battlefield Airmen*, Santa Monica, Calif.: RAND Corporation, RR-618-AF, 2017. As of February 24, 2022:
https://www.rand.org/pubs/research_reports/RR618.html

Robson, Sean, Matthew Walsh, Miriam Matthews, Carra S. Sims, and Joshua Snoke, *Is Today's U.S. Air Force Fit? It Depends on How Fitness Is Measured*, Santa Monica, Calif.: RAND Corporation, RR-A552-1, 2022.

Rostami, Hosein, Hamid Reza Tavakoli HR, Mohammad Hossein Rahimi, and Mohammad Mohammadi, "Metabolic Syndrome Prevalence Among Armed Forces Personnel (Military Personnel and Police Officers): A Systematic Review and Meta-Analysis," *Military Medicine*, Vol. 184, No. 9–10, October 2019, pp. e417–e425.

Rothman, K. J., "BMI-Related Errors in the Measurement of Obesity," *International Journal of Obesity*, Vol. 32, August 2008, pp. S56–S59.

Schuh-Renner, A., M. Canham-Chervak, T. L. Grier, V. D. Hauschild, and B. H. Jones, "Expanding the Injury Definition: Evidence for the Need to Include Musculoskeletal Conditions," *Public Health*, Vol. 169, 2019, pp. 69–75.

Seaverson, Erin L. D., Stefan B. Gingerich, David J. Mangen, and David R. Anderson, "Measuring Participation in Employer-Sponsored Health and Well-Being Programs: A Participation Index and Its Association with Health Risk Change," *American Journal of Health Promotion*, Vol. 33, No. 7, September 2019, pp. 1002–1008.

Shaw, Chris, Keith Abrams, and Theresa M. Marteau, "Psychological Impact of Predicting Individuals' Risks of Illness: A Systematic Review," *Social Science & Medicine*, Vol. 49, No. 12, December 1999, pp. 1571–1598.

Taylor, Natalie, Mark Conner, and Rebecca Lawton, "The Impact of Theory on the Effectiveness of Worksite Physical Activity Interventions: A Meta-Analysis and Meta-Regression," *Health Psychology Review*, Vol. 6, No. 1, 2012, pp. 33–73.

U.S. Department of Health and Human Services, "Table 2-1. Health Benefits Associated with Regular Physical Activity," in *Physical Activity Guidelines for Americans*, 2nd ed., Washington, D.C., 2018.

Vartanian, Lenny R., and Jacqueline G. Shaprow, "Effects of Weight Stigma on Exercise Motivation and Behavior: A Preliminary Investigation Among College-Aged Females," *Journal of Health Psychology*, Vol. 13, No. 1, January 2008, pp. 131–138.

Wheeler, Abigail R., and Joseph C. Wenke, "Military Fractures: Overtraining, Accidents, Casualties, and Fragility," *Clinical Reviews in Bone and Mineral Metabolism*, Vol. 16, November 2018, pp. 103–115.

Williams, Valerie F., Gi-Taik Oh, and Shauna Stahlman, "Incidence and Prevalence of the Metabolic Syndrome Using ICD-9 and ICD-10 Diagnostic Codes, Active Component, U.S. Armed Forces, 2002–2017," *MSMR*, Vol. 25, No. 12, December 2018, pp. 20–25.